Best Year Ever

Thought and Inaction
Through a Long 2020

Brant von Goble

Loosey Goosey Press
Okemos, Michigan

"Best Year Ever" was originally published in *Fleas on the Dog* (2020).

"Avoiding Thucydides's Trap," "The Last Chance Corps," "Student Loans and a Means of Reform," and "The Law Must Die" were originally published on *The Reading Junkie* (2021).

All pieces have undergone significant revision.

Loosey Goosey Press
2222 W. Grand River Ave
Okemos, MI 48864

ISBN: 978-0-9820991-9-3 (Hardcover)
ISBN: 979-8-9853386-1-4 (eBook)
LCCN:2021942259

Contents

Introduction

Fortune is a trickster. Win the *Tremendous Trillions Pick Twenty Superball*, and within a decade, your troubles are likely to stack higher than a Minnesota winter's worth of cordwood. So it goes with *the curse of good luck*.

The curse's chiral twin: Your country is invaded. All appears lost. But your people overcome their differences. Innovation blossoms with the nourishment of bone and blood. By the time the shooting has stopped, you discover that you are richer than you were in the halcyon days of peace.

Put some stock in this possibility, but not too much.

People die. Diseases spread. Some industries prosper. Others are driven to ruin. Victory is rarely unalloyed, and it is never assured. You lose the war, and you and yours stand to be wiped from history at the invaders' discretion. At best, they subjugate you, impoverish you, and force you from your land. To make up for these brutal violations, their descendants name planes and sports teams in your honor. So it goes with losses and consolation prizes not worth picking up from the delivery counter.

Then there is the matter of time. *Today's blessing, tomorrow's curse.* This complicates predictions. There are few easier ways to reduce your reputation to that of *hack* than to gaze into a crystal ball and make unambiguous forecasts for the near future. *Keep it vague!* Such worked well enough for Nostradamus. It might well work for you.

Still, I hazard this: We, the American people, will be *better* and *better for* the experiences of 2020 and the years thereafter, regardless of how matters now seem. Time will bear this out.

And we can improve ourselves and our condition yet more. Strategies and tactics to do so fill this book.

We are more capable than we often believe, and our alleged superiors and nominal leaders, far less. *Our long 2020*—so named after Eric Hobsbawm's *long 19th century*—may well not have finished. But it will. And when it does, we will be fortified as individuals and as a nation, but only if we exert the necessary effort.

And that is on you as much as it is on me. So it goes with trickster Fortune and her questionable gifts.

They are what we make of them.

Best Year Ever
(Sex, Death, and 2020 Vision)

Nothing Happens (Until It Does): Ejaculations of Progress

Fantasize, fixate, pursue, fail (Repeat)

Fantasize, fixate, pursue, fail (Repeat)

Fantasize, fixate, pursue, fail . . .

And then you get what you want.

And it is almost certainly less than what you wanted. In retrospect, the dreams, the chase, the ham-fisted exertions and heavy breathing, and the underwhelming finish will make for good barroom stories and cringe-laugh memories. Or not. Sometimes you are stuck with someone you cannot stand, for reasons that seem less compelling with each additional minute spent staring at that person's shockingly charmless, uglier-than-a-mud-fence visage.

So goes the cycle of revolution. What did you think I meant? And in revolution, even those who see their every demand met are often left with dull victories, shattered dreams, and utopias that end *à la Thomas More*, with at least one person losing his head.[1] *All conditioned things are unsatisfactory . . .* [2]

Since your mind is likely already somewhere below the waist, let us direct it a bit lower, *to the feet*—and the road upon which said feet tread. That road, the road to revolution, is a memorial of sorts, and much like the Kolyma Highway in the Russian Far East, it is built upon the bones of those who gave their labors to it, oftentimes less than willingly.[3] We all walk upon the labors of the dead, but we cannot walk too far along with our metaphor: It has its limitations.

Highways are incremental things, built piece by piece. The road to revolution may be long and slowly constructed, but revolutions themselves do not happen *until they happen*. And *the impossible* becomes *the inevitable*, becomes *the done*. There is no *might*. There is no *somewhat improbable*. Nothing happens. Then everything happens. The revolution takes moments. The consequences last for years. So perchance sexual flights of fancy (and whatever fear of flying thereof) make for a better metaphor than a Russian Road of Bones. Putting aside metaphors, here is the plain truth:

2020 is our year of revolution.

And that is a wonderful thing.

Rather than mourning the world that was, we must let the dead bury the dead. The future awaits. And here is how it will be better than yesterday, which is not to say it will be perfect:

1. We will stop believing the bullshitters.

The *end of history* was the beginning of America's era of bullshit without limits.[4] We had gone on ill-advised escapades before (*Goodbye my darling, Hello Vietnam . . .*). We supported—and continue to support—tyrants who bankroll terrorists (*Hey there, House of Saud!*).[5] And we sold weapons to those who hated us so that we could give money to rapists and murderers, all while claiming to desire freedom and democracy for all of humankind (*Iran-Contra affair? There's romance in the air!*).[6] Our leadership was never wondrously capable or principled unless *capable* is defined as *being born in the right place at the right time* and *principled* is defined as *doing whatever is most expedient at the moment*. Even our great victories—World War II, for instance—were as much the product of America's wealth and geographical isolation (and willingness to accept bright immigrants) as they were any great genius on the part of our leadership.[7] But then, *really smart* people have their parents make their money for them. So perhaps we should give credit where it is due.

During the Cold War, we had some reason to contain our baser instincts—the desire to imprison everything that moves,[8] the impulse to militarize and arm every law enforcement agency to the teeth,[9] and the yearning to obliterate (probably) illiterate herdsmen.[10] We needed to keep focused on the *Red Menace*, which with its strange alphabet, strong liquor, bombastically patriotic anthem, and arsenal of nuclear weapons, was just different enough for contrast.[11] Ideology the Menace had, but mere ideology it was not. Rather, it was a people, a government, and a land that could be easily identified and well-enough understood. We knew where to point our missileers and their missiles.

Since the collapse of the Soviet Union, we know nothing with certainty, so we fish for adversaries, and if we discover there are no fish to catch, we stock the pond. We initiated a *Global War on Terror* (GWOT)—effectively a fight against what is variously *a tactic* or *an emotional state*. This made about as much sense as waging a war against *ennui* (because we should all care about something!), and it fed the piranhas of anti-Americanism the richest and *chummiest* of chum.[12] We found (and continue to find) other enemies and threats of every shape and stripe within our land, be they *superpredators*,[13] terrorist sleeper cells,[14] the Y2K computer bug,[15] or Asian giant hornets.[16]

The dangers of the enemy are always sold hard. Vanquishing said enemy always requires some expensive strategy. The strategy is always either badly designed, poorly

3

executed, or both, and the enemy never does much measurable harm, even when the strategy fails. The failure is always proof positive that more money is needed.[17]

Our leadership is ill-suited to peace. It does not know what to make of it. So it engages in perpetual war, hoping that we will not catch on to its catastrophic belligerence. Our news outlets/content producers do not do much better. *If it bleeds, it leads.* The big six media conglomerates (Disney, TimeWarner, etc.) will do or say whatever they must to keep themselves in the black.[18]

The good news is this: We are more skeptical of these people and institutions than ever before. And our faith in experts—far from absolute even years ago—was further diminished by the great Anticlimactic Pandemic of 2020.[19] Predictions as to the damage that COVID would bring were so inconsistent, so hyperbolic that they put the most alarmist of climate change doomsday predictions—those of the *Day After Tomorrow* variety—to shame.[20] Yet the professionals learned nothing. They will continue to undermine their credibility for a few brief moments of screen time, proving that they are no less inclined to be famewhores than are the rest of us.[21]

If the first seven months of 2020 have established anything, it is that government officials, scientists, and academics know nothing much more than the man on the street. They can do little. They wear no clothes. We are losing faith in the lot of them.

From this good news springs much other.

2. *American moralizing and interventionism will come to an end.*

One of the great global annoyances is the American tendency to save others from themselves—to liberate them, whether they want it or not. We have been doing this for years, but the height of the stupidity was our effort to bring Western liberal democracy to the Middle East. This effort was so singularly doomed to failure that no sensible person would have thought that it had any chance of success. The flaw in the grand plan: the belief that American values are *universal values*.[22] Make no mistake about it, the GWOT was not a war about oil: There would have been easier ways to capture that market, and cheaper too. Rather, it was a scheme hatched by true believers—those who take as inviolable truth that inside of every foreign man, woman, or child, there is a Ding Dong-loving American waiting to burst out (probably because he's hungry).[23]

But this is wrong. It is founded upon the supremely arrogant failure to understand that *they are not like us*. Whoever *they* are, they are not American. They have their values, their traditions, and their priorities—different from ours, but no less authentic or deeply held. We all may bleed red, but not all puke white and shit blue. Anyone who has spent a few years working in another country and away from the expat settlements will recognize the truth in this. And he will soon learn that either he must adapt to *their* (the locals') tempo, *their* values, and *their* way of life, or he must stay indoors, waiting for his labor contract to end so he can fly home.[24]

But despite all their credentials, this much about them cannot be denied: Our gold-plated masters-of-the-universe leaders are *provincial*.[25] They know less about the outside world than does the average soldier or border-crossing day laborer. And their Dunning-Kruger confidence makes them more dangerous still.[26]

And then there is the matter of *human rights*—a fine notion about which all and sundry crow, but that few nations observe except when convenient. If governing a people while respecting their civil liberties with any consistency is possible is a matter yet to be determined.[27]

What *is* clear is that we—the American people and government—are in no position to demand from others what we do not demand from ourselves. Putting aside the past—the nearly genocidal reduction of the American Indian population, for instance—we have no grounds to unhypocritically attack other governments for the treatment of their people *today*.

Do foreign powers routinely abuse, kill, and incarcerate their minorities and their poor?

Of course!

Do they deny their less-privileged citizens fair, speedy, and impartial trials?

No doubt they do!

Do they tolerate inequality of wealth and opportunity so extreme that the difference between the haves and the have-nots is one of universes, rather than mere dollars?

You betcha!

Do they allow the infrastructure upon which their citizens depend to crumble into the sea, leaving only the richest of private-jet rich with safe means of transportation?

Yep!

But what do we do differently?

We incarcerate at a rate unmatched by any existing power. We provide our citizens with the best justice they can buy, and we provide them with roads with free potholes and water with free lead (not *lead-free* water).[28] Our generosity towards our fellow Americans is inversely proportional to our capacity for shambolic crisis-management and political infighting. About none of this should we despair: Our emerging inability to enforce the demand that the world remake itself in our image will save all of humanity lifetimes' worth of grief.

Enforce the demand is not a matter of mere verbiage. Demands we will still make but enforce them we will not. We no longer have the wealth for one international adventure after the next. And we lack the moral stature to have our chest-thumping dictates taken seriously.[29] The more loudly we attempt to boss about other nations and attack their record of ignoring rights and due process, the more impotent we will appear. If we issue a report about the mistreatment of the Uyghurs, the Chinese will tweet back a George Floyd GIF. There the argument is reduced to ineffectual insults. And with each excretion of our holier-than-thou fluff and puffery, our opponents will need only to dig through the public record to make us look to be bigger asses. Guantanamo Bay, Abu Ghraib, the collateral damage of America's many efforts to bomb cave peoples into modernity—our actions and the ready availability of digital images thereof are endless fodder for the meme machines of hostile powers. We can keep arguing the issue— whatever the issue is—but only at an ongoing expense to our dignity.

This all sounds trivial and jejune—tweets and twits and online derision—but it is not. The select shapers of the world hate being teased. They have no tolerance for it. They have been the butt of jokes throughout the ages, but never has the ridicule of the unwashed masses (or other elites) been piped directly into their homes, their phones, and their hollowed-out souls. Enough in the way of psychological attack, and the elite will retreat. They will stop trying to bring about heaven on earth and leave the lot of us well enough alone. God will not save us from *a most oppressive tyranny, sincerely exercised for the good of its victims.*[30] The merciless mockery of the internet peanut gallery will (with a bit of help from America's responsible citizenry).

The pole of global power will shift east, and a different set of values will prevail—less abstraction, less grand design, less individualism, more concrete thinking and emphasis on incremental improvement, and more in the way of collective unity, to be valued above the happiness of the man apart.[31] These *are* values. They are as real as ours, but they are different. A people who sacrifice to get to heaven (us) will view life and its purpose quite differently from those who think more in terms of passing down a legacy from one generation to the next.

One order falls. Another rises. The new world may be less brave than that which we imagined, but it will almost certainly prove more economically sustainable.[32] And we will not bear the heavy burden of trying to make it come to pass.

3. The public will learn to distinguish between science and scientist.

Declining faith in experts need not lead to a rise of primitivism, magical thinking, or technophobia. Rather, just as faith in scientists may decrease, respect for science itself will likely increase. This is good. Science demands no worship. Science demands no faith. Science demands *nothing*. It cannot demand anything. It has no personhood or personality.

8

Anthropomorphizing a process does neither people nor process any service. And the sooner that the public learns how to read and interpret scientific research—how to view it with an appropriately jaundiced eye—the less easily charlatans will be able to bamboozle them. A great many people may indeed lack the intellectual tenacity and capacity to understand the most complex scientific arguments, but that is not to say that they will prove unable to identify glaring errors in logic and experimental design.

The *fundamentals* of the scientific method can be understood by almost anyone, and in an era of freely available information, those who *can* grasp the details and the higher math involved can make the complex simple enough for the majority to interpret.[33] Those who *choose* to avoid this information—who choose ignorance—have only themselves to blame for whatever ill befalls them as a result of them not knowing what they can and should know.

A world in which scientists are valorized is not much better than one in which they ignored entirely. In the latter, their critical warnings go unheeded. In the former, they grow dangerous from an excess of power and a lack of accountability. So it goes with all experts. The unchecked researcher risks becoming another Trofim Lysenko.[34] The unchecked and unaccountable social engineer, an Edward Bernays.[35]

From our skepticism towards experts and professionals, comes another benefit.

4. Our government will become less corrupt and abusive, even as we lose faith in it.

The surest sign of a scoundrel is that he demands perfect faith in his good intentions and rejects independent oversight.

Trust me says the crook, and the wise man grabs his wallet and holds it dear. Experts, officials, and lawmakers who demand that we have high confidence in their goodwill and competence should be held up for special and close examination.

The idolization of authority figures is dangerous for a society, and just as dangerous is an overestimation of the risks authority figures face. This is relevant when considering the role of security services and institutions—the military and police. The narrative Americans have been sold for decades now is that we are under constant risk of attack—from criminals, from terrorists, from immigrants, from our own families.

We are kept terrified of *them*, meaning anyone other than ourselves and our great protectors. We are sold the notion that if the thin blue line breaks, all will turn to hell. Yet for the better part of human history, there was no blue line at all. The first police force was not established in the United States (in Boston, more specifically) until 1838.[36] And before 1800, when France established the first modern police force, *no* country had such an organization in the sense we now take as a given.[37] Before that, constables, sheriffs, night watchmen, elected and appointed officials, and the military all played a role in imposing the law upon the public, but regular policing by a professional uniformed force did not exist. Laws existed, but laws and their enforcers were far less prevalent than today. Despite this lack of ever-present agents of government-approved violence, the historical record does not suggest that colonial America was *Ye Olde Purge*, and to the extent great crimes were committed before the founding of the Republic, they were as likely to have been the *product* of government actions as they were to be *prevented* by them.[38]

Yet a great many of our people, namely White, middle-class Americans, live as though they must cling to the authorities with such a codependent-girlfriend tenacity that being more than ten minutes away from the nearest police station is a terrifying prospect.

These hyperthyroidic, amphetamine-munching felines masquerading as citizens will cling to authority—any authority—so long as there is any left, and when the authority falls away, collapses, or walks off its post to never return, they will cling to the memory and symbols of what once was. But the population of terrified tabbies will shrink. Demographic and economic changes will chip away at it, until it becomes just one more minority, and not a uniquely powerful one.[39] Given time, many of the children of the status quo will turn against authoritarianism, partially a result of campus indoctrination and partially as a result of them earning less while working more than did their parents, and thus being impoverished even in their faith.[40] The emergent groups—poorer, darker, less connected to the established power structure, and more likely to have been on the receiving end of years of destructive social engineering—will prove far more skeptical than did their lily-white predecessors.[41]

They—the replacements—know what most of the world takes for granted: The police are neither more inherently moral nor any more likely to be infallible than any other group of human beings given gun and badge. Ultimately, the police are *men with guns*. And the *hombres armados* (armed men), regardless of how they identify themselves or the values they claim to righteously uphold, are people the *hombres desarmados* (unarmed men) are better off avoiding.[42] Even the most *color-deficient* of us will have a more difficult time denying as much with each new incriminating dashcam, bodycam, or smartphone video.[43]

The irony of this is that the very same technologies that make us distrust our authorities *more* make them *less* likely to do something worthy of distrust. Even judges, probably the *least* likely of any group of authorities to be held to account for their actions, are finally discovering that abusing and tormenting attorneys, plaintiffs, witnesses, and defendants is not a good look on camera. And looking bad on camera can lead to an early (and unceremonious) retirement.[44]

The other great benefit of this—when we see our flaws, so does the rest of the world. The more the world knows of our ways and our failings, the less likely it is to repeat them, which is not to say that other peoples will not make mistakes of their own.

5. *We will quit pretending to give a damn about everything and everyone.*

There is no greater enemy of true compassion than feigned concern. The latter allows a convenient relief of guilt, a saving of face, and not much more. The former—compassion—is more difficult and more limited. We *cannot* care about most things. We *cannot* care about most people.[45] We have neither time enough, nor energy.

The teens (2010-2019) were a decade of great but meaningless display and rebellion without direction. All were well befitting a century in its adolescence. Protests over nothing, about no one, and without any goals beyond mayhem—the University of Missouri and Evergreen State College *happenings*, Occupy Wall Street, etc.—we know about

12

as much about these jamborees of petty destruction as did the participants, which is to say that we know nothing.[46]

But at the heart of all these events was an imperative—that we *must care*. We *must care* about minorities. We *must care* about economic inequality. We *must care* about hurt feelings and emotional and social insensitivity.

And as the years progressed, we faced even more of the same—a never-ending imperative to care. The *Rape on Campus* hoax of 2014, the Kavanaugh hearings, #MeToo, the great demonstrations/riots of 2020—all imposed something on us—that we must make the world *right* according to whoever is doing the protesting and complaining.[47] And we must do our repairing and caring in the most performative, melodramatic manner possible.[48]

The truth is this: Those who *pretend* to care about every wrong, much like those who claim to like all music or all movies or all religions, do not care much about any of them.

This is not to say that we cannot all care about *something* or even several things, but we must, as a matter of necessity, be indifferent to more of the world and more of the people and things therein than not. And those foolish enough to attempt to fix *every* problem on earth, or even every problem in a community of a few thousand, will exhaust and martyr themselves to little effect. As this goes for people, so does it for companies and charities, no matter how large and powerful they may be. We are functionally sociopathic at certain times and regarding certain causes. We must be.

As often as not, wisdom is the art of learning to acknowledge and accept the obvious, rather than denying or raging against it. This is the year we wise up, not because we are inherently sapient, but because we have no alternative. Beat someone about the ears long enough with the truth, and he will eventually notice it is there and that it is giving him a headache.

This is the year we will finally learn to say the magic words: *I do not care. I have problems enough of my own already.* Let us all learn to listen to our inner bastards—the little voice inside of us each of us that proudly proclaims *Screw you, buddy, I will look out for Number One!*

Our lives will be better for this.[49]

6. We will stop apologizing constantly.

A companion to the culture of boundless concern and sympathy—*the apology cult*—is every bit as visible and no less unreasonable. Sometimes for the actions the apologizer has committed, sometimes for the actions of a group in which one is a willful member, and sometimes for being on the receiving end of poor (meaning, somewhat counterintuitively, *good*) fortune—apologies are churned out for every possible reason and come in every form, from the *mea culpa* to the public grovel, to the carefully worded and drafted-by-a-team-of-attorneys variety. Baskin Robbins could never hope to offer as many flavors. What these apologies have in common is this: The very rarely mean much. And even more rarely do they matter.

Apologies, much like a convicted man's alleged remorse for burning down your house and decapitating your pet ferret, fix nothing. Your house will not turn from ashes to wood, and your ferret is no less deprived of his head. And forced apologies— those done under pain of harassment, ridicule, imprisonment, or unemployment—are *worse* than nothing. Coercing one's enemies to scrape and kowtow does nothing more than make the apologizing enemy resentful, the strong and stupid ever more arrogant; and the observant more cynical.[50]

Nothing good comes of this. The worst ritual of the apology cult is the *proxy apology ceremony*, in which those who were not wronged demand (and receive) an apology from those who have not wronged them. This is not an act made in good faith. No one can feel the pain of another, nor is it the right of the living to accept apologies on behalf of the dead. And it is not the place of descendants to presume the attitude their forebears would have assumed in time.

Had they lived a few decades more, the butcherers of American Indians might have concluded that stripping a people of their lives, livelihoods, and lands was wrong. But perhaps not. Given millennia, given until the heat death of the universe, their opinions might never change. They might become no less tenaciously racist or exploitive—and possibly *more* skillful in justifying and excusing their conduct. *Who knows?* And without evidence one way or the other, there is no good reason to presume a particular ancestor-tyrant would be much concerned with redemption.

We would be wise to quit apologizing altogether or to reserve apologies for the most unusual of circumstances. If one feels so inclined to right a wrong, he should fix it to the best of his ability. And if he is not so inclined (or there is nothing to be done), he should neither pet nor kick drowsy dogs, knowing it best to leave them to their dreams of chase and hunt.

7. We will admit that most students learn little and that most children are not special.

Our multigenerational celebration of mental mediocrity—of the perverse and profoundly destructive notion that cognitive weakness is strength and strength is weakness, that no one is simply *a halfwit, dull,* or *about average,* but is instead *special*—is being brought to a nearly instantaneous conclusion by COVID. More specifically, COVID's effects on distance and time as they relate to education are what will make the music stop at this grotesques' ball of fools and self-deceivers.

First, there is the matter of *distance education.*

Distance education has a history of more than a century. Correspondence schools (of the traditional, by-mail variety) go back to the 19th century.[51] And a few of the schools founded in that era are still open. Other iterations, such as learning by radio and television, have been developed and deployed with varying degrees of success. A few, such as the Open University of China (originally *China Central Radio and TV University*), are still in operation.[52]

Computers and the internet have been used to deliver instruction since the 1980s, and electronically mediated courses are common enough today that a large percentage of college students have taken at least a few of them. Still, online learning remains somewhat of a redheaded stepchild. We may tout distance education as a great opportunity for the poor, the rural, the disabled, and the single mother, but Harvard still offers classes in person.

Or it did.

In COVID Land, all the world is not a stage, but a chatroom of planetary scale. This is the year colleges, including the elite ones, kicked their precious, moldable minds off campus quicker than one could utter *homeless undergrad*—community, continuity, and tradition be damned.[53]

Grade schools, middle schools, high schools, trade schools, cram schools—all followed suit. And for the first time in a long time, parents and guardians can now see plainly what their *budding geniuses* are learning *and are capable of learning.*

So, two questions: 1) How much *does* the average student learn? 2) How much *could* the average student learn?

Answer 1: Almost nothing.[54]

Answer 2: Not much more.[55]

It is easy enough to get a child (or increasingly, *an adult*) diagnosed as being learning disabled, differently gifted, *on the spectrum*, suffering from ADHD, or whatever other fashionable ailment was recently added to the Diagnostic and Statistical Manual of Mental Disorders (DSM). There is an entire industry dedicated to labeling and excusing anything and everything— we are fast on our way to medicalizing bad personalities and awkwardness. And any number of clinicians will conform their professional observations to the expectations of those who enable them to continue paying down (slowly, oh so slowly) their student loans.[56]

When discussing learning plans, behavioral management strategies, time accommodations, and medication regimens with teachers, administrators, and clinicians, it is easy enough for parents to think of all this procedurally or bureaucratically —just one more lot of paperwork and protocol. But when the spawn of said parents is plopped in front of the family computer's screen, where said child-beast oozes drams of oils, pints of mucous, and quarts of ejaculate (or gallons of menstrual blood); soils his/her/its pants; and struggles for three uninterrupted hours to correctly recite the first ten letters of the alphabet, considering the *thing* as being much more evolved than the amorphous, eternally suffering blob of "I Have No Mouth, and I Must Scream" becomes a mental exercise only the grandly deluded can long sustain.[57] Thus, it is distance education that *decreases* the distance from parent to child, and in this proximity, delusions die.

Next, there is the matter of time, and how much more difficult it is to slaughter when not in the classroom.

Students (particularly *college* students) who study online may be forced *to study!* No more fighting, no more drugs, no more whoring, no more hugs. Presumably, they can do a fair amount of sexting with their classmates, just as they can have the occasional virtual bar crawl (meaning the students sit at their computers and drink, while periodically punching/ groping themselves at the behest of their peers), but there would be not much in the way of hellraising to be had. Social media still chugs along, but uploading photo after photo of your Instaworthy eggplant grows tiresome for even the most *like- thirsty* of netizens.

And attendance by itself does not mean much in the online classroom, so teachers and students alike must do more than stare at their phones and pretend that education is happening by way of osmosis. Thus, *something* must be done. And once the work product of our nation's bright young minds is revealed, any perceptive, sensible person—parent, teacher, or advocate for education—is presented with evidence of the hugely expensive non-education students receive.

An examination of school coursework and assignments confirms that students *do not* learn much. The students themselves, by their words and deeds, confirm that they *cannot*

18

learn much. This is a bitter pill for many, but the more schools are seen for what they are—babysitting services for children ages 6 to 36—the more we can align their design with their proper function of keeping America's great irritation—her youth—out of our hair and out of harm's way.

8. We will stop paying for bad students to go to worse colleges.

In an era in which information is very nearly free, college is of questionable value. There are a few subjects that require special facilities and equipment—biological and biomedical sciences (about 6% of college majors for completed degrees); engineering (6%); health professions and related programs (12%); homeland security, law enforcement, and firefighting (3%); military technologies and applied sciences (<1%); physical sciences and science technologies (2%); and transportation and materials moving (<1%).[58] Even if we assume a few relevant fields and categories were not included in the National Center for Education Statistics table from which these numbers were obtained, no more than a third of all college students require access to a classroom, a laboratory, a clinical setting, a machine/engineering facility, or a model/experimental farm for them to complete their degrees. The rest can learn the majority of what they need to know to achieve competence in their fields of study remotely or independently.

There is a legitimate argument to be made that some of the never-articulated processes, customs, and procedures required for mastery of any number of domains (*tacit knowledge*, as described by Michael Polanyi) cannot easily be taught or learned by way of self-study or distance learning. But if a student can gain this information in a classroom of 50 students seems no less uncertain, particularly in a climate in which teachers are hesitant to interact with students except in the most cautious, detached, and legally defensible manner.[59]

And there is an equally legitimate argument to be made that some fields simply lack much in the way of tacit knowledge, or that tacit knowledge in many fields (to the extent that it exists) is of so little consequence that students can figure it out on their own. One can imagine a chemistry student learning that a certain apparatus only works properly if manipulated *just so* or a budding biologist learning that certain cultures or cell lines can only be sustained with the most exacting care and feeding. But as one moves from the physical to the abstract, this becomes less relevant.

Once schools move the better part of their instruction online, they face a new reality—that of non-regional (and potentially *global*) competition. Aside from bureaucratic and institutional hurdles, nothing stands between rationally managed higher education organizations and the outsourcing of instruction. Philosophy, mathematics, and critical theory can be taught about as easily from across an ocean as from across the state. Having internationally located teachers educate American students has the potential to save time, money, and legal resources for a school. Consider how many teachers are imported into America's classrooms to instruct students in algebra, statistics, and economics. Sponsoring a skilled worker is difficult. The paperwork can run to hundreds of pages; the delay, to months; and the cost, to north of ten thousand dollars.[60] All this expense and inconvenience can be avoided using readily available hardware and low-cost web services.

Equally great is the burden placed on the would-be professor, who must travel away from his home and all that he knows to work and live thousands of miles away, in a country from which he can be removed if his employment is terminated. Although some travel by choice, others travel by necessity. The latter group would as likely as not stay home, receive their salaries by way of electronic deposit (or PayPal), and spend their income in their motherland—where money may well go further than in the United States.

And given time, change is bound to lead to *consolidation*. Schools siloed within a certain geography can establish near-monopolies on access to higher credentialing, particularly if these institutions provide partially subsidized tuition to in-state residents. When distance becomes irrelevant (for most majors), schools can easily encroach upon the territory of their peers. Colleges, particularly the smaller ones, have been facing financial difficulty for years, with some older (pre-COVID) estimates being that half of all colleges will go bankrupt before 2035.[61] If anything, the COVID crisis will accelerate this trend, quite possibly by a decade or more.

Bankruptcies and bankruptcy reorganizations do not necessarily lead to the destruction of organizations under bankruptcy protection. Institutions can be reorganized, or they can just as easily be divided into sections and sold to pay off creditors. There is also the prospect of schools and universities avoiding formal bankruptcy proceedings altogether by selling assets or merging with larger organizations.

One of several keys to lowering costs by way of establishing economies of scale is for consumers (meaning students, parents, and *employers*) to recognize that colleges are *credentialing* institutions firstly, and *educational* institutions secondly.[62] They serve other functions—as publishers, as research institutions, and as farm teams for the NBA and NFL—but these can all be provided for more efficiently outside

21

of the framework of the university megastructure. In the realm of sports, for instance, independent or community-backed minor league teams could serve the same social and professional function as college teams do, but without being attached to higher educational institutions, which would free them from the legal vagaries of many federal regulations (Title IX comes to mind).[63]

As for the publishing, research, and science and technology training functions of educational institutions—they can be either spun off to freestanding entities, taken over by state governments, fused into regional research consortiums, or sold to larger publishing and research ventures. Whatever happens to these will have little effect on the credentialing division— with that being what processes college students not studying a select number of fields.

So how does this relate to COVID?

COVID effectively shut down every part of America's colleges *except* for the credentialing and financial arms. School sports teams saw their practices and games canceled, university publishing houses slowed their release schedules to a crawl, and laboratories for scientific teaching and research were almost entirely closed.[64] With all non-credentialing functions stripped away, all that is left is an army of bureaucrats in training (and their trainers), staring into screens, darkly.

With the pre-COVID bacchanalia that was college life having ground to a halt, communities losing interest in and connection to schools *sans* football, and many students discovering that they can learn about as well at home without an instructor as they can in a classroom with one, college becomes an unsentimental thing. And unsentimental things can be assessed with no more feeling than one would have for a mutual fund.

In the end, the college degree will either be reformed, abolished, or trivialized. As it stands now, it means little and costs much. Outright abandoning/abolishing the credential as economic signaling mechanism is one way to reduce the debt-burdened carried by young Americans with aspirations of reaching the middle class. Other means to establish the fitness of a young person to enter the hallowed halls of cubicle land would need to be developed. But such is not beyond the realm of imagining.

Trivialization is another possibility. There is no reason that *everyone* cannot have a college degree. Paper is cheap, and electronic certificates are cheaper. This is a more likely terminus of ongoing trends than is the abandonment of the credentialing process. Outright elimination of administrative institutions or procedures is difficult—too many parties have vested interests in maintaining the status quo—however, dilution is far easier to manage.

If enough schools close or consolidate, they will be able to streamline the credentialing process to the point that it becomes not much more demanding or expensive than obtaining a driver's license—hardly an *effortless* process, but not something the average schlub is unable to do. Bureaucracies make liars of us all. Demand enough in the way of paperwork, forms, and sworn statements, and eventually expediency necessitates dishonesty.

And a trivialized credential is a lie—it certifies something that all know to mean nothing. Thus, *almost everyone* may have a college degree by the time all is said and done, but the vast majority will expend little effort and less money to obtain their well-printed wallpaper.

Finally, there is the matter of *reform*. This is probably the most difficult and unlikely path to take. It would entail a radical rethinking of decades' worth of college design and development that goes back to *Griggs v. Duke Power Company*.[65] The credentialing and educational aspects of a college can easily be separated. The issuance of certificates of compliance and docility—the reason an obvious majority of students attend college—can be done in other, less-wasteful ways. And as for the monkish and peculiar few—those who want nothing more than to think critically and at length—the liberal arts model of education can be allowed to blossom as never before.

Schools, no longer burdened with the task of serving as gatekeepers to the neo-mandarinate, would be free to help the curious pursue their interests and learn abstract reasoning. Since almost all books and educational content (such as lectures) can be found online, this—the new, improved, non-credentialing college—would need to serve as a community and gathering place, its purpose being to promote thought and discussion, rather than to hammer varied minds into a uniform shape.[66] Such a simplified model will allow for tremendous decreases in administrative overhead.

The arts, humanities, and social science divisions of colleges will become more similar in purpose and operation to private, interest-specific learning centers, such as music and dance/ballet academies and hobby learning centers for ceramics, painting, or wilderness survival. Given that these private ventures will be both less expensive and less regulated, the quality of their instruction will vary from world-class to no better than the (appalling) present state of affairs.

While market forces should keep the number of bad and overpriced schools to a minimum, some students of the humanities at these institutions may be duped. This happens from time to time in the world or martial arts training, yet the sky has not fallen. The difference: The defrauding of the former (humanities students) is less likely to lead to serious injury than that of the latter (martial arts students).[67]

Either way, we (the taxpayers) will not be funding private academies for philosophical debate, so what happens therein concerns us little.

The transition from the hodgepodge of credentialing, research, publishing, and athletics that now defines the university to more streamlined and purpose-built replacements will not be complete by the end of the year, but the COVID crisis has accelerated this great and long-overdue process. Soon, there will be little reason to send masses of marching morons to the nearest state center for indoctrination and soul destruction.

9. We will learn to stop worrying and love the robots (and remote work).

Generations of easy living may well have caused horrific decay in the cognitive capacity of the average *first worlder*, but that is not to say that we have quit learning altogether. The lesson of 2020—a hard taught one—is this: *Stop worrying about jobs. Stop worrying about your fellow man. Love the robots.*[68]

Fifty years ago, our neighbors were *neighbors*—nearby humans we knew as individuals. Twenty years ago, they were *the people in the house down the street*—we might not have known them personally, but we could recognize them on sight.

Ten years ago, they were *whatever lives over there*—we might not have known or recognized them, but we suspected that they were alive: *Something* had to be turning on and off the lights and ordering pizza.[69]

Now, the aforementioned are either potential disease vectors, or communists, feminazis, anarchists, or MAGA-monsters-in-training—whatever terrible things that go bump in our respective nights. Even when we knew those around us, we might have not cared much for them: *Familiarity breeds contempt.* Today we drop the pretense. We no longer need to pretend to care about their jobs or incomes. And human interaction has become an albatross around our (surprisingly anti-social) necks.

All this liability, complication, and risk of disease or death makes staying home (and minimizing human interaction) more appealing than it was even a few years ago. And liability hurts employers as well. Employees get sick, employees sue, and employees risk embarrassing whoever cuts their paychecks.

Automation has been industrially and economically relevant for generations. Robotic welders and surgical assistants are already used so frequently as to be almost unworthy of attention.[70] Since the 2004 DARPA Grand Challenge (when a self-driving car was first able to complete the 150-mile course), self-driving cars have been slowly but steadily improving, and Tesla's most recent production vehicles are only a few software upgrades away from reducing the human driver to a legally mandated seat warmer.[71]

Grocers, retailers, and warehouses are also gradually dispensing with human shelf stockers, loaders and unloaders, packers, and cashiers.[72] Considering the size and severity of COVID outbreaks at major retailers and in Amazon warehouses, accelerating the replacement of man with machine seems prudent. And then there is the matter of demands for higher wages. *Fight for 15*, which has been chugging along since 2012, has had some success. Given the increasingly left-wing/pro-labor/anticorporate tenor of a great many 2020 protests, these demands are likely to grow louder, more persistent and of greater effect.[73] This makes unskilled labor more expensive—and automation comparatively cheaper—than it would be otherwise. So we will have more and better machines replacing those workers who will not (or cannot) work 24-hour shifts in virus-filled, stadium-size, un-climate-controlled death boxes (er . . . *fulfillment centers*).[74]

And then there is COVID-accelerated growth of remote work. Slightly more than 50% of American adults would prefer to work primarily at home, and nearly 75% of Americans would appreciate the option to work at home at least occasionally.[75] Not all jobs can be done this way, but many of those that cannot are steadily being automated away or transformed into jobs that can (telehealth and remote surgery are just two examples of the latter). COVID led to a huge increase in at-home work, and there is compelling evidence that the end of travel and distancing restrictions will not reverse this.[76]

Each of these trends—the growth of automation and the expansion of distance work—reinforces the other. The more robots, of the entirely autonomous or of the human-guided variety, the greater the percentage of labor that can be done from home. And the more people choose to stay at home, the more relevant delivery and service robots become.

As Millennials have come to dominate society, the *fear of missing out* (FOMO) has been replaced with the *joy of missing out* (JOMO)—the pleasure one takes from missing the many inconveniences of socializing and of steering clear of those one would rather avoid.[77] There is nothing new about wanting to keep one's own good company. What *has* changed is the role of technology, which makes being a cheerful loner all that much more cheerful, and COVID. For the first time in living memory, the American imperative of *get out more* has become that of *for the love of God, stay home!* And best of all, keeping to oneself is no longer a sign of being damaged or dangerous, but one of being *a responsible and self-sacrificing citizen.*[78]

The extrovert went from fantastic to foolish, feckless fleabag, and the introvert rose from suspected pervert to known patriot.[79] This great shift helps not only the shy and the retiring; it benefits all living things. The average American adult drives more than 13,000 miles per year, and the country consumed 3.39 billion barrels of gasoline in 2019.[80] Although some of this is used for purposes other than fueling cars and motorcycles (powering lawn equipment, off-road vehicles, and small planes), cars are the primary consumer. If the average car and motorcycle mileage rates are cut in half by way of remote work—not an unrealistic assumption—a billion barrels of oil could be saved every year, and more than 10,000 lives could escape premature termination by way of vehicular accident.[81]

As for time spent commuting, the average American dedicates a total of 19 workdays worth of time driving to and from work every year.[82] Assuming workload and efficiency remain constant, every person who transitions from working in a cubicle to working at home gains the equivalent of three-weeks' annual vacation.

Finally, there is the added benefit of transparency. There are few better places to hide from work than an office. Exercise and bathroom breaks can burn through a few hours a workday, but relying on such tactics is the hallmark of amateurs and peons—those bound to lose. The real *lords of time destruction* make more money, have better titles, and exert even less effort than their inferiors.

Achieving victory in the war on productivity requires a sophisticated attack on all things temporal. The first weapon: *the meeting*. The second: *the email*. And those who most deftly wield these two can achieve almost perfect uselessness (and be promoted for doing so). Nod along, repeat a few key phrases, project enthusiasm and energy—while committing to nothing in particular—suggest that any idea or course of action be given a meeting of its own, and you have mastered the meaningless meeting.[83] But this is a mere rusty saber in comparison to the Gatling gun of the excruciating email. Here is complete user's manual:

1. Find some task or question to address.

2. Compose a missive about said task or question.

3. Add between 20 to 50 irrelevant tangents.

4. Reorganize the text so that it appears coherent but lacks any discernable meaning.

5. Helpfully invite the recipient to contact you if he or she has any questions or requires any clarification. (Rest assured that the recipient will.)

6. CC at least three other people, just so that they can be *kept in the loop*.

The saber may slice time into paper-thin strips, but the excruciating email does one better—it annihilates time so completely and renders it so thoroughly dead that DNA and dental records are the only tools sufficient to identify the remains.[84]

But these weapons are less effective on the home front of the home office. Video conference calls may be riddled with technical problems, but the awkward and delayed nature of the interaction that occurs therein discourages time wasting. Their *inefficiency* and *unnaturalness* demand that all participants be both more *direct* and more *efficient*. This *seems* paradoxical, but it is not much different than that which caused telegrams and text messages to be short and to the point. One can ramble in person for hours, but when paying by the word, the communicator tends to get to the heart of the matter.[85] Granted, the cost of interacting by way of Zoom is only a fraction of that of sending a telegram (and easier on one's thumbs than sending a text message), but little delays here and there make speaking for the sake of mere idleness more trouble than it is worth.

Then there is the matter of doling out assignments. The remote worker submits an assignment on time (or not), and the work is acceptable (or not). The specifics of the task, the time spent working, and the quality of the work are all there—digitally recorded and open to review. Claims of *assisting, inspiring, or motivating* the worker are hard sells. Objective measurements of worker productivity are easier to make when computers track everything, leaving less open to subjective interpretation.[86]

The people who are most likely to be hurt by difficult-to-falsify performance metrics: middle managers. But they are, at least as often as not, in the way, their *people skills* and red staplers be damned.

10. We will innovate faster than we did before COVID.

Medical science moves at a snail's pace, and the pace has grown slower in recent decades. This is partially the product of the increasing complexity of treating a great many of the remaining diseases (with the low-hanging fruit having already been plucked).[87] It is also a result of differences in work style and legal norms. A great many of the significant human studies of yesteryear could not be conducted today. The entities responsible for reviewing and approving research protocol (institutional review boards) would either revise these research designs to the point of uselessness or ban the experiments outright.[88] And the approach to scientific and engineering research used from the beginning of the Industrial Age to NASA's heyday was almost suicidally reckless by modern standards. The origin story of powered flight was not much more than a series of poorly controlled crashes and explosions, with the first fatality happening under the watch of Orville Wright himself.[89] The development of nuclear fission and medicine and rocketry was no better, with the latter claiming human and animal casualties alike.[90]

The low-hanging fruit problem may not be easily addressed, but the matter of risk aversion will almost certainly be transformed by COVID and the public, governmental, and private reactions to it. Although COVID has proven relatively mild in its effects on public health (as far as pandemics go), its spread has already spurred better and faster sharing of medical/genetic information among nations, advancements in public health and treatment protocols, and almost shockingly fast vaccine development.[91]

Outside of the medical field, famously sclerotic institutions, such as law schools, went from very nearly refusing to acknowledge the distance learning paradigm to embracing it wholeheartedly in a matter *of days*.[92] Even the court system— one of the most rigid and self-important institutions in existence—has seized the opportunity to work from a distance. Judges may not care how much of a burden one pointless hearing after the next imposes on poor and disadvantaged defendants (or how much time, money, and heartache these defendants could be saved by way of technology), but they embrace the modern at lightning speed when they fear their wellbeing may be imperiled by a coughing convict.[93]

As COVID-shutdown economic and cultural complications ripple through our society, the institutions that do not change will die (as they well should).

11. We will finally recognize how many Americans want to watch the world burn (and why).

We should have seen this—the current political instability—coming: President Trump, regardless of what one thinks him, was not elected by an army of the undead nor by aliens. Rather he was chosen by millions of Americans. Some bought his pitch for Making America Great Again, some hoped he could slow the nation's slide into senescence, some had faith in the Christian piety of a twice-divorced Manhattanite billionaire, and some wanted lower taxes. Many simply disliked him *less* than they disliked the other team, but a fair number saw him as *an agent of chaos*—a meme-making bull with a Twitter account in a china shop nearly half a continent in size.[94]

Too many dismiss this last factor—*the chaos vote*—as being of no consequence, or pigeonhole it, as though it can be fairly described as *left*, *right*, *radical*, *Antifa*, *Marxist*, *racist*, *incel*, or some other convenient term that suggests a cohesion of belief as understood by the average sociology, psychology, or political science major. There *is* cohesion of sentiment in this portion of the electorate. But what binds this lot together is more nebulous and more frightening than what the average man and woman of comfort and privilege can easily grasp. Worse yet, it is far more *universal*.

Media and policy institutes are either dumb regarding the source of nation-destroying rage or do a fine job of playing the part, mocking those who are not happy to have their communities and families destroyed and their lives commoditized by the chosen few. No matter how badly these elites (left and right) mangle what they claim to be intent on improving, they and their mouthpieces will not frankly speak of the errors they have made.

To the extent any acknowledge that the unwashed masses have any grounds for dissatisfaction, some may profess a vague sympathy for the Black Lives Matter protests. But only the rarest of the rare managers, professionals, and social engineers would take any responsibility for undermining the Black household and the Black middle class through a toxic combination of poorly designed social welfare programs and job-destroying free trade policies.[95] This privileged ignorance is more than annoying to the non-oblivious, it is *dangerous to the entire country*.

Black families and communities have been destroyed. White ones have as well, with but the smallest delay. *Fury, detachment, disconnect, and nihilism* may manifest in different ways in different communities, but they are not specific to any one race, religion, color, or creed. And until the deliberate unknowing of cause and remedy is corrected by a skillful instructor, our society will only continue to become less stable. This year *is* that dear teacher, and she is giving wayward students the vicious beatings and stern guidance they require.

Art imitates life, imitates art. Consider the breakout film of 2019: It foreshadowed 2020 so closely as to be unnerving. An examination of its underlying message and how radically it contrasts films of even a few decades prior reveals much of the new American psyche.

Joker—a tragedy about a man who tries to be funny— resonated far more effectively than one would anticipate in a society of prosperity, peace, and relative safety. Nothing about the world of *Joker* is aligned with the physical world of the present. Our cities are not totally overrun by massive rats. New York City (upon which Gotham is clearly based) is less 1980s punk hellhole than it is gentrified playground of the superrich. There are few (petty) criminals in the City That Never Sleeps— they cannot make rent. And the Marauders of Manhattan do not pick pockets and violate damsels. They drain entire economies and rape nations, and they would rarely stoop so low as to pluck a Patek Philippe Grand Complications up from the sidewalk—doing so is not worth their time. Mugging such peons as are the lot of us would be beneath their villainous dignity.[96]

Joker is not materially realistic. It is drab. It is about a difficult, psychologically damaged man who has been abused and betrayed by the few people who have seen fit to notice him and who has been ignored by all the rest. Arthur Fleck—the clown who would become Joker—has more in common with the nameless protagonist of Gogol's "The Overcoat" or Dostoevsky's *Notes from Underground* than he does with a character sprung from the mind of Steinbeck, Melville, or more modern writers, such as Stephen King.

What Fleck and his unnamed Slavic compatriots in the Kingdom of Despair share (and that separates them from most

34

American protagonists) is worse than the absence of friends—it is the lack of a specific enemy. Captain Ahab had his whale, King's protagonists have their supernatural opponents, and Steinbeck had his well-defined social wrongs. To have an enemy can be better than not—at least those who do can aim their energies in a named direction. Fleck is deprived of even the small comfort of having someone to hate. Rather, he has *everyone* to hate in general and *no one* to hate in particular. There is no reason for him to *not* hate anyone, and much reason for him set the world aflame. And although Arthur might never comprehend it, his feelings are more than the result of base and destructive instinct; they are part of an evolutionarily sound reproductive and survival strategy.[97]

The problem is not that Fleck enjoys his time alone—that he appreciates solitude—but that he has no one and nothing at all. This is fundamentally different. No friends, no enemies, no purpose—and Fleck's consolation prize is uncontrollable, joyless laughter and a few petty tormentors.

The only way the Arthur Flecks of the world stand much chance of having success is if the existing power structure decays to such a point that entrenched people and systems break. Only then—when all is up for grabs—may they have some small chance of getting more than the *absolutely nothing* to which they lay claim at present.

What else do these men—Fleck and the Slavs—share?

They are so injured and so fragile that kindness would be at least as likely to destroy them as save them—one can kill a long-starved person with too much food, offered too quickly.[98] Anything more than a bit of passing, carefully calibrated humanity towards them would likely put them on high alert: They would not (and could not) know what to make of such a thing. There is not much anyone can do for *Fleck, etc.* that does not involve superhuman effort. This is the most disturbing aspect of their (and *our*) predicament: Few would be very much inclined to help any of these men—they are not lovable and aiding them would do little to burnish one's reputation—and even those who might, would be hard-pressed to find any measure or medicine that had fewer side effects than benefits.

And *Joker* was a 2019 film. Turn back the clock a mere two decades (1999). The top five films in the United States were *Star Wars Episode I, The Sixth Sense, Toy Story 2, Austin Powers: The Spy Who Shagged Me*, and *The Matrix*.[99] Granted, *The Matrix* was a filmic metaphor about the process of unshackling oneself from the conventions, deceptions, and mental slavery of modern life. And *Fight Club*, an iconic representation of disconnect from the consumerist world, was released that same year. Yet *The Matrix* and *Fight Club* share a different (and hopeful) heart that *Joker* does not. Neo breaks free from the Matrix. The unnamed protagonist of *Fight Club* eventually liberates himself from his alter ego and annihilates a nation's worth of debt. Even at their darkest, there is always Hollywood Hope and Happy Endings™ in these films of yesteryear.

But for Arthur Fleck, hope is not an option—the light at the end of the tunnel is the possibility of being drugged into catatonia (at worst) or escaping an asylum to punish the world that punished him merely for existing. *This* is what resonates— the feelings of a man without connection to anyone or anything. Such hollow ringing sounds no better in one time or place than it does in a different one. It has little basis in racial or acculturated prejudices. It can be described no better in one language than in another. It is general in its appeal and relatability. And although ideology can *harness* the energies of the Flecks of the world, namely by giving them a sense of place and purpose, it cannot eliminate them. And even this harnessing is of limited effect and duration.[100]

One can make too much of movies—sad, happy, mind-numbingly stupid, grandiose, and romantic films have been made in different ratios since film left the phase of train-crash shorts. But the difference between box office boom and box office bust tells us something—something of the temperature and mood of a people. Turn to television and consider this: How well would *Friends* land in the 2020 zeitgeist? How well would *Breaking Bad* have done in 1997?

One can also make *too little* of the arts or treat them too narrowly. Not every Arthur Fleck is White, thin, and living with his mother. Some are in financially stable positions. Some have prestige. Those who want to set a match to it all are oftentimes poor (or not), frequently poorly educated (or highly educated), White (or Black or Brown), and rural (or urban or suburban). They may be single, or they may be married or divorced. Many are men, but a considerable percentage are women. Academia houses a fair number of them—those who howl against the world in journals so dry and obscure that even their editors, who undertake the (largely unpaid) labor of wading through one Foucault-referencing manuscript after the next, struggle to do any more than skim these texts before they go to press. One can be respected, tenured, and well-paid and still be without a true friend in the world.[101]

The desire to deconstruct (and sometimes *dismember*) an entire culture is seldom felt by those who consider themselves meaningfully joined to it. Those who perceive themselves as having a place of some value within a community may see its

37

flaws and work to correct them, but this is a matter of *improvement*—of remodeling the house or adding rooms—not tearing it to the ground.

So now we must concede that we have a problem—one that 2019 showed us in film and 2020 has shown us in the streets—that cannot be easily remedied.

And this is great news!

Not that something like 24% of Americans would like to watch the country be leveled by nuclear blast (or incinerated by more conventional means)—there is little cheering in that fact.[102] Rather, the *good* is that the despair, the pain, and the isolation felt by millions of Americans is now impossible to deny.

Since 2000, we have been *Bowling Alone*. Now we burn our cities down together.

Fleck, the Slavs, and the discontented poor (and not-so-poor) share this: Their world has *already* been turned upside down once. *Notes from Underground* was written when Russia was integrating into the West. The values and traditions of the people were being swept aside by the winds of technological change (the Industrial Revolution) and crushed underneath new thoughts and philosophies to which few could quickly adapt.[103] Likewise, the discontented poor have had the customs of their ancestors—dictating everything from the role of the family to the role of the employer to the nature of relationships between men and women—derided, replaced, or made irrelevant. Their better-off (and equally frustrated) peers have seen much of the same.

We have come to expect an entire class of elites to live entirely in the world of theory. For the most select of the most select—those with a great bent towards metaphysics—such a life is nearly the platonic ideal.[104] But only a peculiar few have the mental buoyancy to remain afloat when waves of ideas come crashing down on their heads as though they were boats off the coast of Kanagawa. For the rest, this is a miserable way of drowning.

We all too quickly forget how much tribe and clan ruled our lives until what was, in the scheme of history, moments ago. We have *tried* to replace these with radical independence, which would work well, if only the better part of the population proved capable of critical thought and self-determination with little in the way of guidance from family, community, or elders. Such has not proven to be the case. This is too much for the average man or woman, and most of the supposedly exceptional cannot fare much better.

Even amongst the most intelligent, there are not many adventurers, and an adventurous spirit, as well as raw cognitive ability, is what freethinking requires. Free and critical thinking also requires a willingness to attack one's ego throughout life— to admit that the thinker may be wrong about nearly anything and everything, including dearly held values—and this process of ongoing creative destruction is unpleasant. It is unpleasant because it demands the slow murder of the old self and its replacement with the new. Here is the paradox: One cannot fully become mentally independent, with self-formed thoughts, values, and beliefs, unless he is willing to demolish himself. Only through this can he pull down and away the thoughts suggested to him by men he has never heard of, who have taught him that the rubber stamps of established beliefs and doctrines are somehow his own.[105]

The sooner we acknowledge this—that we cannot blow apart the worlds and lives of hundreds of millions and expect them to be anything but angry, injured, hateful, and vulnerable and that *they cannot* construct workable selves without the help of others—the sooner we can set things right. The select few must devise a common set of beliefs, suitable to most, that will allow the better part of humanity to function sustainably. *Only* the select can correctly oversee the construction of communities founded upon something other than fury, pain, mindless hedonism, or the collapsing shell of family. The select must toil to design something new if anything of durability is to rise from this era of bad concrete, carelessly poured.

A different metaphor: We cannot simply repave the old road. It cannot take us where we need to go. Nor can the building of new roads be left to those with an exclusively commercial interest in doing so: All such people and businesses will do is engineer highways that lead to prosperity and power for themselves at the awful expense of the many. This task— that of studying the old ways, including both those that failed and those that succeeded, assessing the needs and resources of the billions, and of then building something that works— stands to be one of the great challenges of the coming decades. Those who can think and who can reason for themselves and others will have little choice but to undertake this extraordinary task if they wish to have a habitable world. Otherwise, the Arthur Flecks and their companions will only grow more destructive.

The conventional experts can do little to contribute to this endeavor—they are too self-assured in their ways to see their failings. So the species must rely upon the few, the proud, the free thinkers who are willing to labor on, despite the scorn of both the indifferent and the ignorant. And the lone reward the thinkers are likely to receive is knowing that they are the engineers of the roads and the turners of the world.

Some of them will rise to this occasion. This is the year they will see the need, the year that their ingenuity starts to get the best of them. They will not fix what is broken because they *care about everything*, but because they are builders of peoples, myths, and spirits, and they can no more abide disordered societies than can a musician of the highest caliber abide the sound of a poorly tuned instrument. The freethinker, both despite *and because* of his ongoing and well-controlled self-destruction, is the bulwark against the entropy of the universe.

12. We will learn to recognize both the inevitability and necessity of death.

And yet, death is the destination we all share. No one has ever escaped it, and that is how it should be, because death is very likely the single best invention of life. It's life's change agent. It clears out the old to make way for the new.—Steve Jobs[106]

America is awakening from the dream of the evermore— from the notion that our institutions will never die, our way of life will never be replaced by another, and our citizens will never fracture into incohesive factions or be swallowed by another faster, stronger, smarter, or meaner people. We have our share of survivalists and doomsters, but they are no less attached to the American dream than are the rest of us: In their minds, the collapse of the nation either precipitates or will precipitate the collapse of civilization itself.

Decline and decay are rarely so fascinating. Governments fail, currencies collapse, but life goes on, with most people doing as they have always done—trying to make their way through the day without irritating the men with guns.[107]

We are not the first to develop this hubris. Stefan Zweig's *Golden Age of Security* encompassed several decades of Pre-World War I history, in which his homeland of Austria was prosperous, progressive, and placid.[108] If not *the end of history*, Zweig's era was the end of dramatic, violent, and destructive history—all replaced by technological innovation and steady improvements in living standards and human rights. The parallels to late-1990s America are difficult to ignore for all but the most unmindful.

Turning to the present: much of the stability we take for granted will pass. And this is as it should be. Aging governments and ways of life are bound too much to rules of different eras. Sustaining them can only be done by strapping the nation down as its muscles gradually atrophy. Such was the approach that the Qing Dynasty took to controlling China, which went from the country with the world's largest economy to one under the heel of drug-peddling, big-nosed invaders in the space of a few generations.[109]

To predict that America will undergo a period of declining global prestige and decreasing global involvement and significance and to predict that American lives will improve involves no contradiction. Two decades of war in the Middle East and Africa have proven costly, and by letting die the dream of a world in which all peoples and values are perfectly in harmony with our own, we can effectively enrich ourselves to the tune of trillions of dollars.[110] And billions will hate us less than they do today. Rome conquered the better part of Europe, but the Eternal City is not under perpetual attack by Goths or Gauls demanding freedom. Old grudges are forgotten, and old wounds heal in time. In a generation, such could be the case with the United States and the Middle East. The desert peoples may never like us, but if we leave them alone, they will cease to think of us much one way or the other.

And then there is the death of the individual. We can sustain the fantasy of unlimited medical care and resource expenditure for all only so long as there are no crises.[111] We have avoided the question of who lives and who dies by throwing money at everyone. But this does not always work. There are hard decisions to be made. Refusing to decide is a decision of its own.

We were completely unprepared to decide who received a respirator and who did not, so luck, panic, and emotion made the decision for us. We, as a nation, *decided* to let irrationality rule. But we were lucky. The next virus might do more than save Social Security a few dollars here and there. So now is the time to weigh our values carefully and decide how we will mete out life and death.

Death comes bearing gifts, first among them, *the imperative*—the sense one has that the minutes, hours, and days are irreplaceable and should be used deliberately, lest they go to waste. There are few better cures for procrastination than a terminal diagnosis. And a terminal diagnosis is what we have all been given from the moment of conception, even if we forget as much. Our ever-growing bureaucracy, our monstrous system of credentialing—one that discourages the competent from engaging in skilled and professional work and that favors the plodding—and our infantilization of children until they are nearly in their middle years: Death will solve these problems. It sweeps out the old and broken. It makes room for the new. It impels those who would be waiting in line forever to the front.

Finally, there is the matter of those of us who will be rendered useless by the fast-approaching changes. The middle manager, the petty social engineers and technicians—what can and should be done with these people? A few will leap into the abyss. Others will fight change with all their might. Others still will cause trouble of varying degrees or join the ranks of Fleck and his fellow travelers. They may be good students and highly trained, but the displaced will not be much better equipped to find purpose in the post-2020 era than is the average cart pusher. They may be worse equipped in some ways: Their work is their identity. Most cart pushers are not so burdened.

Those who cannot keep up with the march and the rhythm of the world are unlikely to simply get out of the way. The thinkers must consider these people too and find a place for them until Death drags them from their desks, screaming.

Hindsight, Foresight, and Perfect Vision

The world after 2020 will be different from the one before it. Every day is different—a statement so obvious as to be cliched—but different differences are . . . *different*. Watching a puppy grow into a dog is one thing. Watching a caterpillar transform into *Mothra* is another thing entirely.

A technological singularity—the Industrial Revolution— already happened.[112] The next one will happen faster. There is nothing new about singularities. They are just weeks where decades happen or years where millennia do. Foresight is limited in normal times, and even hindsight does not afford us 20/20 vision. We can only see the slightest ways past singularities—they warp the light around them—but that is better than seeing nothing at all.

Now, we turn back to how this missive started—with sex and death. Each necessitates the other, and we shall see plenty of both. The latter—the death of the old things and ways and people—will hurt, possibly even more than we fear. The former—the messy, the unhygienic, and the frequently awkward creation of the new—will be less enjoyable than we hoped. This is the year that the new will be conceived (if not necessarily born). This is the year that much that should have happened long ago finally does.

This is the best year ever.

Avoiding Thucydides's Trap
(Theory, Tactics, and a Call to Action)

Defining the Elite, Theories of Conflict, Theories of Control

The rise of China is inevitable. The decline of the American empire is no less so. This constitutes the greatest shift of global power in several hundred years. All we—the American people—can do is choose how to respond to the foreordained. Without action on our part, starting now and continuing until the geopolitical rebalancing has progressed to the point of absolute incontestability (which will almost certainly occur by 2035), the American elite are bound to engage in extraordinary and counterproductive violence to preserve the position the empire affords them. This piece will examine different means of controlling human behavior, some based on Positional Insecurity Theory, others based on Substitution Theory, and others still based on Distraction Theory, and explore their relevance to the problem at hand. By applying strategic monkey wrenching informed by these theories to annoy the baddies—the elite—we may well prevent a great catastrophe, have fun, and humble those who would level the world.

Overproduction of the Elites and Thucydides's Trap

Before going into abstract reasoning, two major theories must be briefly explained:

Elite overproduction/overproduction of the elites[1]—when a society produces more candidates for positions of power and prestige than it can employ. Peter Turchin, the developer of this theory, has argued that this has the potential to lead to political instability as competition for elite status grows fierce.

46

Thucydides's Trap[2]—described by Graham Allison and named after Thucydides, an ancient Greek historian and general, is the tendency of an established and an emerging power to go to war when they have overlapping regions of hegemony. Within this text, it will refer exclusively to the potential for such a conflict to happen between the United States and the People's Republic of China.[3]

How these mechanisms stand to amplify each other and what can be done to address the potential problems arising from this amplification must be examined.

The National Elite and the Threat They Pose to the World

Positional/Foundational Statement

The American elite, particularly the national elite, are incompetent.

They are unable and unwilling to learn from their mistakes.[4] They are overconfident regarding their expertise, their virtuousness, and the universality of their values.[5] They are profoundly ignorant. And despite their alleged differences in ideology, national elites on the left and right have more in common with each other than with their plebian fellow political travelers.[6] The elites are raised in nearly identical environments (although in different cities).[7] More importantly, they share a capacity for self-worship and overestimation of their worth to society. At least some of them are well-intentioned, but they will not take kindly to losing their prestige and power, and they will feel entirely justified in using any means at their disposal to protect their inheritance. After all, they are *the best and brightest* the world has ever seen, and the best suited to lead, so by guarding their position of authority, they are doing the entire world a favor (or so their reasoning goes).[8]

The American people must be aware of the hazards of the elite mindset and behavior and actively work to prevent these egoists from causing great harm during the current global power transition. China's rise results, not from any failing of the West (although Western trade policies accelerated the rate of change), but because China has a demonstrated ability to resume its historical role of superpower.[9]

This is the position taken throughout this text. Those who disagree would be well advised to stop reading. There is little here of value for them.

That the American elite are dangerously unqualified to lead is supported by at least five decades of evidence. Consider this short and incomplete list of some of the many failures of foreign policy devised by the national elite:

1. (1953) The Central Intelligence Agency facilitates the overthrow[10] of the duly elected Iranian government of Mohammad Mosaddeq and his replacement with the less-than-loveable Shah Mohammad Reza Pahlavi.[11] In theory, this was supposed to help a United States ally—Great Britain. In practice, it led to the establishment of an Iranian theocracy under the even-less-loveable-than-the-unlovable-tyrant-before-him Ayatollah Khomeini, [12] and Iran became one piece of the tripartite Axis of Evil.[13]

2. (1954) After complaints from the United Fruit Company— a powerful force in politics at the time[14] with a major presence in Central America—the CIA initiates Operation PBSUCCESS, with the intent to remove Jacob Árbenz, Guatemala's second democratically elected president, a

leader who is in favor of higher wages and widespread suffrage (with *higher wages* being what draws United Fruit Company's ire the most).[15] Árbenz is quickly replaced with Carlos Castillo Armas, a violent dictator who does not long remain in power. After the fall of Armas, the country plunges into a civil war, one in which more than 200,000 people died. On the plus side, Americans probably enjoyed several years of *slightly* cheaper bananas.

3. (1961) The Bay of Pigs invasion, an attempt to overthrow the government of Fidel Castro, occurred. The anti-communists, trained and equipped by the CIA, were captured almost immediately.[16] In theory, the invasion was supposed to remove Castro from power. In practice, the United States government lost the conflict and provided the Cuban government with 53,000,000 USD (or about 442,142,000 in 2021 USD) of food and drugs for the release of more than 1,000 fighters—an exchange that almost certainly would have been perceived as a victory by the communist government.[17]

4. (1960s and onward) The CIA made more than 600 attempts on Castro's life.[18] In theory, he should have died many times over. In practice, Castro ruled Cuba for almost 50 years.[19] He died at the age of 90, probably from extreme old age.

5. (1955-1975) The United States engaged in conflict throughout southeast Asia. Generally called *the Vietnam War*, a more accurate name is the *Second Indochina War*,[20] as significant military action (namely bombings) occurred in Laos[21] and Cambodia,[22] rather than in Vietnam exclusively. In theory, the government of South Vietnam should have remained a stable force of democracy

in the region, providing a bulwark against communism. In practice, the Republic of Vietnam fell, Operation Menu—the bombing campaign against the Khmer Rouge—failed,[23] Cambodia descended into an ideologically driven purge that killed between 13 and 30 percent of the population,[24] and Laos became a communist nation in 1975.[25] The United States lost against the Reds *three times,* and the human cost of this folly was great: The Second Indochina War resulted in at least one million deaths [26] and approximately 800,000 refugees.[27]

6. (1980s) In an effort to fight *an evil empire*, the Reagan administration financed the mujahedeen in the Soviet-backed Democratic Republic of Afghanistan.[28] Weapons, including the Stinger anti-aircraft missile, were provided to radically conservative Muslim groups.[29] One of the few inarguable victories for the CIA, the United States' involvement in Afghanistan achieved its goal of collapsing the Afghan government[30] and forcing the Red Army to withdraw from the nation.[31] It had the secondary effect of allowing one of the most oppressive and violent regimes in recent memory—the Taliban—to take charge.[32] It also facilitated the rise of Osama bin Laden and left the country awash in high-quality small arms.[33]

7. (2001-2021) The United States invaded Afghanistan to overthrow the very same bastards it helped install a few decades ago. The Taliban quickly fell, but a viable alternative to it was never established. After approximately 20 years of combat operations[34] and more than two trillion USD in expense,[35] the United States has decided to withdraw, with there being a high probability that the Taliban will return to power within a matter of months.[36]

8. (2003-2011) The United States invaded Iraq[37] to look for apparently invisible weapons of mass destruction[38] because the U.S. had recently been attacked by terrorists from Egypt, Lebanon, Saudi Arabia, and the United Arab Emirates.[39] The Iraqi government fell almost immediately, which led to the capture of leader Saddam Hussein (perhaps not a former ally in the strictest since, but whose 1988 nerve gas attacks on Iranian troops were aided by American intelligence services).[40] This was as intended. The resultant power vacuum facilitated the rise of the Islamic State of Iraq and the Levant—a government at least as reactionary as that of the Taliban.[41] Presumably, this was not as intended.

All the actions described thus far have been international. *Perhaps*, thinks the open-minded reader, *the American national elite have less talent for creating ideal global outcomes than they do for effecting the changes they desire within their nation. After all, one is likely to understand his people better than he does others.* This is sensible thinking.

It is also wrong.

Consider the *successes* (as they were) of the elite within the United States. The welfare state and America's horror-show-quality public housing[42]—both developed and promoted by D.C.'s big brains—*may* have led to an increase in the number of children born outside of intact families.[43] In synergy, these systems *certainly* contributed to the establishment of vertical hellscapes[44] more often found in developing nations.[45] Efforts at forced racial integration of schools led to extensive White flight[46] and astounding wastes of money[47] (and probably the further impoverishment of the inner cities). And reform of the educational system has made colleges and universities into centers for ideological training[48] and learned helplessness[49] that would put the most skillful of Manchurian brainwashers to shame.[50] These are but a few examples of the failings of the managerial class. The complete list of elite-sponsored catastrophes is so long that attempting to condense it within a single essay is impractical, although a few people have made honest efforts to do so.[51]

The difference between a strong chess player and a weak one is not in the player's ability to determine what effect a good move would have on the board at the time the move is made: Those with no more than a few hours' training can understand the advantages of capturing a queen. The difference is in the ability to *predict*.

The best players do not see 20 moves ahead, despite some claims to the contrary.[52] Given that one's opponent is likely to have three or four viable options from which to choose at each turn, thinking about every possible progression of moves for more than about a dozen steps would be computationally impractical for most computers and far beyond the reach of the human brain. Rather, the skilled player thinks about only the *most likely sequence of moves*. This requires foresight, and it requires developing an understanding of the perspective of one's opponent. *It requires pragmatic empathy.*

Even a mediocre chess player will assume that the opposing side has some *will*—an aspiration to win—and considers the strength of his opponent's desire, but the absolute worst chess player will take nothing of the sort into account. He will think *no* steps down the line. The board is seen as still life. And he will regard his foe as inert. The dolt will make *no* effort to know his enemy,[53] with each of his adversary's moves presenting an entirely new board and new problems to the spotless mind of said eternally sunny simpleton.

This is the level at which our national elite play. They are blessed fools—blessed because each day is entirely new to them, with whatever misfortunes that befall them being either the result of bad luck or the dastardly dullards who fail to recognize the greatness of (self-declared) incandescent intellects. *If only the world would play along with our game and let us win (as it should!), all would be well!*

This is a happy way to live—right until it lands you in the tomb,[54] the prison cell, or the poorhouse. Even when avoidable misfortunes come to pass (and they will), the American elite will forever take comfort in their unwavering belief that they did nothing wrong.

And this mindlessness is why we cannot leave the world and its turnings to them.

Definitions

Elite is an inherently broad term. It suggests excellence or prestige, but such a description leaves much undefined. The most significant limitation is that it does not distinguish between *context-dependent* and *context-agnostic* elite status, thus failing to separate those who are elite within a competence-evident domain (an elite marksman, an elite welder, an elite chef) from those who are members of *the elite*—a social caste.

Within this text, *the elite* refers to the latter—those who derive their prestige in society from their affiliation with the structures and institutions of legitimate power, rather than due to evidenced skill or ability. To further remove ambiguity, *the elite* and *the elites* will only be used to describe those whose function within these institutions is to control society at large, either by way of direct commands (as an executive, commander, or judge would), policy decisions/policymaking, or modulation of the official narrative. They are generally trained in management, business, social sciences, journalism, or law— fields that are far removed from the natural and material worlds—although some may have other types of training that they rarely use, except to enhance their credibility. Thus, a highly regarded neurosurgeon—*an elite physician*—is not to be regarded as a member of *the elite*, whereas a policymaker with a background in neuroscience (from the right school, of course) likely would be a member of *the elite*. The first is a skilled mechanic of the body. The second, a manager who, one hopes, understands science.

The elite and *the elites* overlap with Chomsky's *New Mandarins*, with the greatest difference being that *the national elite/elites* within the present text only refer to the highest levels of that class.[55] Of course, *elites*, much like samurai, Freemasons, and European nobility, are all assigned rank according to rules that are as complicated as they are opaque to outsiders. All established elite, regardless of standing, have a vested interest in maintaining the existing institutions of legitimized violence—and this includes everyone from the assistant prosecutor of Bumpkin-Semiliterate County to the members of the United States Supreme Court to a senior researcher at a D.C. think tank to the editor of a national newspaper—but only a few have (and can have) true prestige and the authority to change policy, rather than merely enforce it with varying degrees of selectivity. And it is upon those select few, *the national elite*, whom we primarily focus.

The only other categories considered within this text are *insider/established elites*—those who turn the wheels of power as they please—and *outsider/overproduced elite*—those who have been trained at the same prestigious institutions as are the established elite, but who have never been allowed to spin any wheels of size or consequence. This difference—that of having power or not having power—gives these two groups opposing goals—a point critical to understanding several of the tactics developed throughout this text.

Foundational Assumptions

The assumptions on which this document is grounded are that:

1. The American national elite, as described above, will lose much of their power and prestige over the coming decades as the American empire and American institutions decline.[56] The elite are aware of this as a *possibility* but do not yet consider it an *inevitability*.

2. This eventuality described in the first assumption can be neither stopped nor substantially delayed, as it is the result of both irreversible global economic shifts and long-unaddressed tension within the American power structure.

3. The national elite's efforts to delay or reverse these trends are likely to be destructive to this nation, many other nations, and the elite themselves.

4. The national elite's response to signs of declining power will be one of desperation, not rationality. Thus, they cannot be counted upon to moderate their aggression without *external* guidance and manipulation.

5. The most demented and feverish response from the national elite would entail both expanding the already-

underway assault on the rights of the American people[57] and initiating a shooting war against Mainland China.

6.   The only people capable of containing and controlling the frantic viciousness of the destabilized national elite are a dedicated few of the American citizenry. Without their efforts, the worst-case scenario—a prolonged land war in Asia and a violent civil conflict at home—may well be realized.

7.   Redirection of energy[58]—both by way of induced confusion and by way of the promotion of (metaphorically) fratricidal behavior on the part of the elite—is the safest, surest, and most ethical means to prevent both serious civil disorder and a third world war from occurring.

8.   To avoid a calamity during the transition period of unipolar to multipolar world the American citizenry must do nothing more than buy time. The elite need not be kept preoccupied indefinitely, only until they have no choice but to realize their coequal (if not inferior) position relative to the elites of other nations. Once they are unable to deny that their time has come *and gone*, they will have no rational or emotional incentive to foment wanton destruction.

9.   The tools required for the task at hand are available to the American people. They have only to use these tools wisely and practically to protect themselves, their nation, and the world in this time of metastasis.

The informational and theoretical underpinnings of these statements are the subject of a portion of this text. How to turn them into an actionable plan constitutes the remainder.

The Nation-Destroying Risk of Thucydides's Trap

Thucydides's Trap has been set. It has only to be sprung. And the American national elite are uniquely likely to plant Lady Liberty's foot in said Trap due to the mechanisms from which they derive their power and the vulnerability of these mechanisms to attack and decay.

Modern America—highly industrialized, technologically advanced, perpetually mobile—is a recent invention, and we may easily forget how little history is behind it. The United States before the Second World War was so radically different from the United States of today that it cannot be regarded as the same nation. Before the War, the country was a regional power. It had a presence in the Philippines,[59] but its role in determining the outcome of most world events was relatively minor. Britain's empire—including Greater India, Hong Kong, Australia, Canada, and several smaller territories—vastly exceeded the size and importance of anything controlled by the United States.[60]

American industry, infrastructure, and cuisine—these were either built up to support the War,[61] built afterward to prepare for *another* war,[62] or so radically remade during the Second World War that what was once homespun and organic became stable, consistent, and ready to be dropped into a rucksack and consumed as needed.[63] And the present-day American mindset, culture, clothing, cities, and *people* have been so reshaped by the War and the industries of war that it is difficult to imagine anything even vaguely resembling the nation as it now stands having formed without the perceived imminent threat of extermination or invasion.

This puts the post-Cold War national elite in an unenviable position. What previous generations built, was built to kill, preferably something big (hence a massive nuclear arsenal[64]

and weapons systems designed for industrial-scale conflicts).
Yet since the USSR collapsed—leaving only a constellation of
minor countries, the names of which no God-fear American
would even attempt to pronounce; vodka; tough guys in track
suits;[65] and Putin-riding-bears memes[66]—the national elite
have been at a loss. Stalin went out for a pack of *Herzegovina
Flor*[67] and a liter of kvass[68] decades ago and has not returned.
His suitcase seems to be missing. *Wait . . .*

Daddy has abandoned us!

And the current crop of elites was deprived of an enemy/
father in their tenderest years.

So they have daddy issues. And their daddy issues are *our*
daddy issues. This is worse than them just taking up with some
middle-aged, spray-tanned record producer their mothers
rejected in high school and who takes Tom Leykis's[69] advice[70] a
bit too literally. This is seeking out every problem, every
nightmare, every terrorized and tearful moment of youth and
endeavoring to recreate it on a never-ending loop.

The need to have an enemy to define one's purpose is part
of the human condition.[71] It is limited to no one nationality, age,
race, sex, ideology, or religion. Still, *the intensity* of this desire
is greater for some than others. And much of what we want and
psychologically expect is the result of what is familiar to us. The
modern American elite are not defined by centuries of heritage,
nor are they defined by ancestral connections to the land. The
elite are not *viscounts*, *lords*, *barons*, or the descendants of
noble warriors—they are technocrats. Their nominal fields of
expertise are large-scale human mobilization, industrial
production, and management grounded in psychological and
sociological theory.

Unfortunately for them, the current crop of national elites are not particularly adept at any of the aforementioned This is partially due to generational decay (generations of easy living making for lower average levels of performance),[72] partially due to complacency, and partially due to policies they deployed against the American people and (indirectly) themselves.

Outsourcing the production[73] of critical supplies;[74] relying on immigrants as skilled workers,[75] rather than training their fellow Americans; and promoting political education and time killing[76] over substantial education in the second and third-tier schools that *should be* readying the technicians who keep an industrialized society running—these gave the national elite short-term power and profit, but they also weakened their long-term position. When work is outsourced, control of the workers is outsourced as well. When immigrants replace local workers, they bring with them values, perspectives, and loyalties that make them behave differently from multigenerational Americans—not always a bad thing.[77] And immigrants often have family bonds and traditions[78] that make atomizing their communities into loosely affiliated clusters of perfectly malleable and perfectly isolated consumers difficult.[79] Finally, there is the matter of the *Revolution of Culture* within the schools for the subordinate classes (lower managers and regional elites). The same ideology that allows the national elites to justify their cyclical deconstruction and reconstruction of the national mindset and the diminution of their forebears' legacy has inevitably been turned against them.[80]

If every part of American life is corrupt, toxic, abusive, and shameful, why should the nation's institutions—including the structure of authority and legitimized violence—be spared the destruction that all corrupted things so richly deserve? And if the privileged are inherently bad, and degree of privilege corresponds with degree of badness, are not the national elite the worst of all?

From the perspective of the elite, the most terrifying aspect of impossible standards of purity is that they may someday be applied to (against!) those who devised them.

The effect of rapid deindustrialization—promoted at both the corporate level and the policy level by the national elite—is to make the position of the elite more precarious, their mindset more embattled, and their behavior more dangerous.[81] The transfer of technology and industry to other countries (namely China) [82] accelerated the development of global economic competition. It had the additional effect of displacing the working class and compelling its members to either resign themselves to poverty and addiction, in which case they retain little incentive to invest in society,[83] or to climb atop the credential treadmill and attempt to join the ranks of the managerial and symbolic-information-processing semi-elite.

This has tremendously increased credentialing pressure and inflation at every of society level.[84] It has quickened the overproduction of the elites and ballooned the conglomeration of citizens who are deeply dissatisfied with the national elites and elite power structures,[85] who are disconnected from the civilization and indifferent to its survival, and who are opposed to the continuity of America in its present state on ideological grounds.

Almost every action undertaken by the national elite over the last three decades has advanced the decline of the United States, enabled the rise of somewhere else, and weakened the elite's ability to lead by way of inspiration, rather than sheer force or fear.

Stated another way: The national elite have hammered the steel of happenstance and their unearned good fortune into Thucydides's Trap. Likewise, the overproduction of the elites is the result of unforced errors on their part. Given that these outcomes imperil them, they likely did not desire for such to occur. They almost certainly intended the opposite—to strengthen themselves and their position. Thus, we have observationally established that the elite are inept within the domains of global and national strategy and likely to shoot themselves (and America) in the foot while intending to shoot their enemies and challengers in the head.[86] If this is not proof enough that these people need to be disarmed, nothing could be.

The American national elite are bunglers of the most appalling sort—the sort that *cannot* see the legion errors of their ways—and that makes Thucydides's Trap of present global concern. A wiser, more mature, and more sophisticated elite could have delayed the rebalancing of global power. An even reasonably competent elite could orchestrate a graceful passing of the torch—during which the American people could see their standard of living *increase* due to reductions in grossly excessive military spending;[87] the elites could preserve their power within a reasonable sphere of influence; and the dignity of the Chinese and American government, power apparatuses, and people could be preserved. This would be so easy to arrange that one needs either great malice or *active and profound ineptitude* to force any other outcome.

Lamentably, there is much evidence that the national elite are *inexpert experts* (or *expert at being inexpert,* depending upon one's preferred phraseology). We, the dedicated and responsible few, must prepare accordingly. We must act as though our inaction will lead to the greatest of disasters, bombs and all.

Violence and Positional Insecurity Theory

War is a mere continuation of policy by other means.

—Carl von Clausewitz, *On War*[88]

When one is in a position of absolute and unquestioned authority, there is not much need for violence. The capacity for violence must exist. The *instruments* of violence may well be present. But not every bodybuilder has punched someone in the face (most probably do not—such would take time away from their fitness and diet regimens), and a great many swords never leave their scabbards, except when in need of a good polish. *Absolute power has an (almost) absolutely deterring effect.*

Likewise, when potentially adversarial powers have established effective and non-overlapping boundaries for their authority, violence is greatly reduced, even if the organizations establishing these boundaries have reputations for sadistic brutality. Thus, regions in which gangs have well-defined turf have less violence than those in which battles for blocks and corners are ongoing—this being one reason the Mexican government has established checkpoints to keep different gangs and associated vigilante groups out of each other's territories.[89] This general observation about positional and resource/boundary instability and violence can be scaled down to the level of the interpersonal just as easily as it can be scaled up to the realm of the international.

Interpersonal violence has been on the decline in Europe for more than 800 years.[90] And America has gotten consistently safer since the colonial era.[91] There is no epidemic of *interpersonal* violence in the United States. America's infrastructure[92] and cities[93] may be crumbling, but one is less likely to die at the hand of another in them than at almost any other time in history.

The theories for this are as numerous as they are incomplete.

More than one person has argued that America's *tough-on-crime* approach[94] has done much to make the nation safer. This is suspect. First, the available research suggests that the relationship between harsh punishment (three-strikes laws, mandatory minimums, etc.) is weak.[95] Second, crime has dropped throughout the developed world, with most European nations (such as Norway) not having implemented policies anything like those in the United States.[96]

A different idea (popularized in *Freakonomics*[97]) is that increased access to abortions led to many potentially violent people being eliminated before they were born.[98] Another is that the elimination of lead from paint and gasoline resulted in fewer people being born with behavioral problems.[99] Another still suggests that the increasing average age of the population of the developed world—and the resultant smaller number of young men—has resulted in less violent crime.[100]

The abortion argument seems logical enough, but Ireland, where abortion was illegal until 2018, has both homicide and rape rates far below those of the United States, where abortion has been legal decades longer.[101] This does not disprove the abort-the-future-con theory, but it does cast some doubt on it.

The lead-reduction argument is intriguing, but difficult to evaluate on a global scale, with lead-reduction and abatement policies varying widely across the globe, and it does nothing to explain a drop that began in Europe *before automobiles were invented.*

And the age-increase hypothesis likely has some truth to it; however, it does not entirely explain why the current generation of young people are less likely to commit crime than were those in their age group decades ago.[102] Nor does this explain why teen pregnancy rates have dropped throughout the United States.[103] Fewer teens would make for fewer teen pregnancies overall, but such would likely have nothing to do with the rate of teen pregnancy in an age cohort.

While any of these theories stand to be at least partially correct, none of them can entirely account for the recent decrease in violent crime. Of course, they may work in concert, which does not negate the possibility of yet another civilizational shift being relevant.

Rather, I would propose a simpler argument—a major reason we are less violent is that we have less need on a personal level to engage in violence to maintain our position in society. This is not so much about prison and punishment as it is about providing alternative routes to resolving disputes of position and resource access and about *greater access to resources in general* (greater abundance/reduced scarcity). We are less likely to need to engage in violent struggle to obtain essential resources (food, etc.); to obtain/maintain social rank/position in a community, tribe, or team; or to gain access to *forms of amusement* and *ways to dispose of our surplus time.*

The last does not obviously follow from the evidence and hypotheses thus presented, but that makes it no less worthy of consideration (as will be done in a later section). Unfortunately, our non-violent methods of positional and resource conflict resolution work imperfectly on a personal level. On the class, national, and international levels, they are even more inconsistent in their performance.

And a problem unique to the issue of resolving class-entry and class-gatekeeping questions (meaning determining who gets the coveted class positions in a society) is that these positions in the higher classes are *inherently finite*. Technology has very nearly eliminated hunger in the developed world, thus making battles for food quite rare.[104] It has increased access to entertainment, thus reducing competition for amusement. It has exponentially added access to communications and knowledge, so much so that even working-class Americans can easily afford to communicate with working-class citizens of any number of developing countries daily if so inclined. Access to even the highest quality information has followed a similar trajectory, and this pattern is likely to continue so long as the price of communications bandwidth continues to drop, as it has for more than 30 years.[105]

Medicine, corrective lenses, photography and imaging systems, synthesized micronutrients, publishing technologies, and artificial lighting—innovation can provide abundance of many forms, but regarding status, it can do little. The closest it affords is the creation of new, interest-specific virtual communities, in which one can achieve some prestige through knowledge, competence, presence, or dedication. Still, this does not provide *more* status. New technologies enable us to cut the status pie into thinner slices, but they make the pie no bigger. The pie *cannot* be made larger than a certain size. Communication can be democratized. *Being superior* cannot, as *elite status* (within this text) is something one has because of who or what *one is*, not because of what *one has done*. It is the *being elite* that gives one's opinions weight and credibility, *not* the strength of one's arguments and reasoning that makes one's opinion special and that allows one to join the ranks of the elite.

Thus, conflict for status is a gnarly problem. No matter how many improvements in life quality are afforded by technology, the quest for elite status dictates that participants in the status market go bigger (as in buying *giga-mansions*[106] on the West Coast) or that artificial scarcity be imposed—that being a major reason that Harvard, despite having an endowment of more than 40 billion USD,[107] has a total enrollment[108] smaller than that of a state school[109] with an endowment less than 1/8th the size.[110]

The second problem worthy of note about the status gatekeeping system is that it must be *perceived* as having some relationship to the worth of those assigned positions of power. This is a trait common to all social systems. In an earlier era, hereditary titles and positions were tolerated (at least in part) due to the fatalistic belief that one's merits are determined by station of birth—*from good blood comes good men*—and that ancestry or the gods will cause those who *should* get power to have it.[111] The truthfulness of this belief is less relevant to the strength of the elite than is the widespread *faith in* its truthfulness.

Technical competence can be independently verified, as can natural fitness (strength, speed, beauty, etc.), but deservingness to rule over others, especially at the abstract, policy level, is almost perfectly untestable. Off the battlefield or the playing field, much of the relationship between executive decisions and outcomes is difficult to ascertain. Thus, elites, the national elite most of all, must have the implicit confidence of at least some of the people (the enforcers of their rules, if no one else) if they are to be more than the objects of resentment.

In a nominally meritocratic society, buy-in to the myth of earned status is critical.[112] The elite can point to neither their ancestry nor the grace of their deities to justify their powers, so they must instill faith in the *institutions* that declare some to have won the competition for power and others to have lost. Without the societal presumption that government, schools, and businesses will pick the good over the bad, not only is the credibility of these systems undermined[113] but so is both the willingness of the people to obey[114] the elite and the people's inclination to put forth the extra effort that makes such a society uniquely productive.[115] If respect for the power-granting structure collapses, the institutions will be despised, those granted authority will be ignored or mocked, and the populace will stop trying to win what they recognize as a rigged game. Finally, those who are peripherally connected to elite systems but not fully accepted by them (a group discussed in the next section) will grow increasingly likely to destabilize these systems by way of developing alternatives or by striving for the destruction of the present systems with no concern for what will replace them.

This describes the present situation in America to a T.

The shortage of elite positions, an overabundance of elites, and the conflict that arises from as much were considered by Turchin. The utility of this conflict and the means to exploit the weaknesses of the belligerents, however, is untrod and fertile ground.

Positional Violence, Overproduction of the Elites, Thucydides's Trap, and the State of Emergency

67

Positional violence is not inevitable on an interpersonal level, nor on the level of the state. There are simply varying incentives and disincentives for armed conflict, the ratio and nature of which change over time. With few exceptions, wars and great acts of violence are not initiated by the peasantry. Rather, they are begun by the elite, with international conflict being more the domain of the *established elite*[116] and internal conflict being more the province of the (often provincial) *outsider/overproduced elite.*[117]

To fully understand this, one must consider the overproduction of the elites and Thucydides's Trap from the perspective of positional violence. Overproduction of the elites is most likely to lead to intranational (or intra-empire) manifestations of positional violence. Turchin, the developer of the elite overproduction model, sees disorder and violence resulting from elite overproduction as a negative, but that is not to say that it cannot be put to positive ends.[118]

In contrast, Thucydides's Trap is a state-level outwardly directed (*international*) embodiment of the same human tendency towards positional violence demonstrated by the *battle of the elites*, but on the level of the nation-state.

It is at the intersection of these two that we may find either war or peace, depending upon our volition.

Elite intragroup (civil) conflict can occur at the same time as intergroup (international) conflict, but they tend not to because both civil strife and international armed engagements consume similar resources, hence the Russian withdrawal from the First World War.[119] Still, the relationship is more complex than *external conflict = no internal conflict* or *internal conflict = no external conflict*. Civil wars—largely fueled by positional struggles between the established and

68

outsider elites—demand a nation's full attention, but the *threat* of civil war may make external conflict *more* likely if the established elites believe that a common enemy will force the people of a nation (outsider elites included) to put aside their differences for a common goal.[120] Muscular interventions on the part of the state are also more likely to be tolerated and sometimes welcomed in times of external threat.[121] And these interventions include methods to coerce or silence all who challenge the status quo.

It is no accident that America has been in a state of permanent emergency for nearly two decades. Since the *Global War on Terror* began, the state, as directed by the established national elites, has grown ever more extensive in its reach, both at home and abroad.[122] And as the number of un- and underemployed college graduates—a group chiefly consisting of those who were trained to join the American mandarinate, if only at the lowest levels—increases, so has the government's power to surveil, manipulate, and coerce under the flimsiest of pretenses.[123]

So long have the alarms of invasion and panic been ringing that we are nearly deaf to them. Thus, new alarms have been installed. Russian hackers,[124] COVID-19,[125] the North Korean cyber army,[126] and who knows who and what else—the threats just keep on coming, with most of them proving less fearsome than the terror-porn delirium that heralds them, which is not to say they are entirely harmless. The problem with this desensitization is that *more* alarms are not enough. Each alarm must be *louder* than any that came before. Given time, this begs for war, not against a state or rebel group armed with nothing more than rusting Kalashnikovs and diarrhetic goats, but *a real enemy*—one who can fight a *real war* against us. Perpetual escalation is the long-term cost of the permanent emergency. Escalate enough minor problems, and at least a few of them will cease to be minor.

Thus, the better part of discouraging the positional violence instigated by the elites—namely that taking the form of activating Thucydides's Trap—is that of timing. There is a danger zone in which a nation is most likely to fall into the Trap. This region of greatest hazard lies at the nexus of elevated (but not extreme) elite contests within the nation and the rising of a new global power concurrent with the falling of an old one.

It is only in periods of transition or immediately before or after them that state-sponsored positional violence is likely to serve the elites well. Once the time of transition has completely passed, normalcy will return.

If the fratricide of the overproduced and established national elites can be disciplined and regulated by responsible parties, the chances for reducing carnage to a minimum are good. This possible engine for peace was mentioned at the beginning of this text, but how to elicit the needed behavior will be explored later.

Now that we have considered Positional Insecurity Theory, we will turn to Substitution Theory and then Distraction Theory. Finally, we will consider how all these theories can be applied to the manipulation of the national elite to render them less dangerous than they are at present.

The Needs of Mankind: Substitution Theory and Its (Dis)Contents

What does one need to survive?

Food, water, protection from the elements—the necessity of these is self-evident. The need for community—common to

70

almost all people, regardless of social rank—is implied in Positional Insecurity Theory. *Without community, social position means nothing.*

Finally, one needs amusement. The last may not seem to be a *need*, but without it, life becomes so difficult to bear for so many that they are likely to become destructive, either towards themselves or towards others, if not both. And such is profoundly dangerous to the health of a person so afflicted and the things and beings around him. Thus, we turn our attention to this previously unexplored matter.

Violence and Time Abundance/Violence and Amusement/ Violence and the Tribe

If the *male warrior hypothesis* is correct, the greater part of male intrasexual violence has been for access to women.[127] From an evolutionary standpoint—given men's relatively high degree of reproductive elasticity and the winner-take-all outcome of male sexual competition—this makes sense. And lensed through our modern understanding of reproduction and science, we can even see this as existential issue—men without children were unlikely to leave much of a legacy before the advent of the city-state.

Without dismissing the significance of reproduction to the psyche, it is important that we not attribute modern knowledge to ancient ancestors. Although humans likely developed an understanding of the relationship between sex and the birth of offspring long before the development of written language, exactly when this happened is impossible to say.[128] To someone in the natural condition of ignorance, how one leads to the next is not obvious. Not all sex results in pregnancy, and the delay from impregnation to its outward signs would further obscure the connection between the two. And there is no reason to assume that primitive people saw the *primary* purpose of sex as being reproduction. A great deal of sex had today is more for entertainment than to pass down one's genetic heritage. Our ancestors were likely of no purer heart.

From the perspective of man in the most primeval state (and animals in the state of our pre-human ancestors), sex is not about reproduction, it is about the satisfaction of an urge for an activity that is not necessary to sustain his life—*For the most primitive man, sex was a form of itch scratching, entertainment, sport, and a way to pass the time.* In learning and culture, we have exceeded the primitive man by orders of magnitude. In instinct, we are not much different.

We may well philosophize about the importance of family, generativity, and the noble bonds of nation, but our base nature cares not for these grand ideals. We *desire* comfort, social relationships and position, and amusement. We desire a tribe.[129] We and our desires are barbarians at heart. The extent to which we understand these desires does not much change our tendency to act upon them. Consider how many otherwise capable men have thrown themselves to the wolves for the momentary pleasure of sexual congress. It is doubtful most such men were thinking about their legacy—of either the genetic or historical sort—when penetrating Penny, the perpetually pleasant (and perennially pregnant), punctually present paralegal from Pennsylvania.

Intelligence has only a moderate effect on overcoming the instincts of man. Knowledge has not much more. If anything, they allow one to indulge his animal desires in more destructive ways—the ignorant idiot lusting for power and respect may kill a few here and there. At most, he may terrorize a school's worth of innocents[130]—but the man of intelligence, education, charm, and ambition can torment and oppress an entire nation until his insecurities are resolved (or he grows tired of killing).[131] And if a considerable amount of research is to be believed, we (as a species) may be less intelligent now than we were a few thousand years ago, when interpersonal violence was nearly as much the norm as the exception.[132]

When considering *why* the world is a more peaceful place, we should bear in mind the limits of intelligence and knowledge. We have already considered decreases in violence from the perspective of reduced positional conflict as well as the role both abundance and systems of arbitration have played in making the world safer. This reduction in violence can also be considered from another angle—that of Substitution Theory—with the knowledge that what the modern world provides to sate our appetites is oftentimes quite different from what nature and tradition afford.

Time Substitution and the Necessity of Entertainment

Despite the ever-growing list of physical,[133] mental,[134] and environmental[135] limitations and concerns facing us and the loss of so much of what we have long assumed necessary to maintain an orderly civilization—intact families,[136] traditions, shared values, national culture,[137] a sense of connection to place,[138] community, and religion[139] —we, both collectively and individually, survive without great difficulty. A noteworthy percentage of what we *thought* a people and a nation required to function has proven to be, like the hapless barista and the hard-drinking realtor of 2020, *nonessential.*[140] This observation does not establish that we *thought* wrong, only that what we once may well have needed, we now no longer do.

Rather, we have excelled at creating *substitutions*—a significant number of them *preferable* (in at least some ways)

73

to the things they have eclipsed. In a nation where more than 40 percent of adults are overweight, it is difficult to argue that our foods are neither sufficiently plentiful nor sufficiently delectable.[141] They may be faker than prostitute's protestations of love, but they are *real enough*. The same *good-enough-ness* goes for simulated combat and the virtual teams/community of the gaming world.

One of the more interesting correlations in crime reduction and technological development is between that of the release of the first PlayStation and a drop in youth hooliganism—with the latter occurring a few months after the former.[142] Playing a drug dealer in *Grand Theft Auto* may not be as exciting as beating the streets with little baggies in hand (or in Carhartt jacket, more realistically), but given consistent declines in adolescent drug-use rates, it certainly appears to be more popular.[143]

Finally, there is the matter of *sex*, which if not *the* primary motivator of male excess economic productivity, is a major historical factor.[144]

Yet in an age and nation where sexual restrictions and taboos have very nearly vanished, American men are becoming less sexually active by the year, with a growing number of them having no sex at all.[145] And they seem fine with this. Apart from marijuana, they use fewer drugs than they did a decade ago,[146] and they are not uncontrollably violent.[147] The unattached and underemployed have proven to be of no great threat to modern society. This—the hollowing of the truism that young men without sexual access, life structure, or externally imposed purpose are dangerous to themselves and others—is a technological feat too little observed and far too infrequently lauded.

Pornography serves as a partial alternative to meatspace fornication and sexually aggressive interaction,[148] and online ersatz relationships [149]—the sort one might have with an OnlyFans girl—are growing more popular.[150] But one should not think of sex as a discrete and irreplaceable thing, but as one of many low-tech forms of entertainment to have been pushed away by the great waves of digi-ero-info-engagement.

Thus, we can see how technology has allowed for the substitution of the natural with the unnatural in four domains of concern: 1) essential resources[151] (food, etc.); 2) social rank and position[152] (this substitution has many limitations); 3) community[153] (which closely relates to social rank/position); and 4) amusement/surplus-time disposal.[154]

And all these substitutes are more *entertaining* than that which they replaced: This may well be the greatest accomplishment of all. The same technologies that have so effectively placated the peonage (*peonage* meaning *most of us*) can be applied to pacifying the elites at every level, including the national elite, although these technologies will require substantial modification in their design and usage.

Substitution Theory Summarized

Substitution Theory is a theory that dictates when, how, and to what extent one thing may replace another.

Despite their triumph over the real, the substitutes considered are not perfect replacements for that which came before them. Modern food *might* be an improvement over the low-technology predecessors of a few generations ago—at least if one is to consider declining rates of serious nutritional deficiencies,[155] such as those resulting in goiter[156] and scurvy.[157] As for the other substitutions, they are almost all *thinner* than their predecessors. They lack the complexity and depth of the pre-technological alternative. Online communities, game-based or otherwise, entail less complex interaction[158] than do physical communities (with their reliance on body language, etc.). Virtual social status is more fragile than more organically developed alternatives. And online relationships (and pornography) are less physically stimulating than their meatspace counterparts. The *thinness* and the *entertaining nature* of these substitutes do not counteract each other. Rather, they make them addictive—a useful characteristic for our purposes.

From an examination of their successes and failures and their strengths and limitations, one can derive a condensed *Theory of Substitution*:

> *A substitute designed to meet a basic human want or need will supplant its predecessor to the extent it is* good enough *for a specific purpose to provide a reasonable degree of satiation; is at least as reliable in its operation as that which came before it; and is sufficiently cheaper in terms of time, money, risk, and energy. It need not provide every feature of the original, nor need it share a common construction or lineage with that which it has displaced.*

> Degree of substitution *may vary across domains, with the substitute entirely usurping its predecessor in one domain, partially in another, and negligibly in a third.*

And here is an Economic Corollary of Substitution Theory:

> *Those who control access to the substitutes have great power. They will retain that power so long as their product remains market competitive.*

And here is a Critical Caution of the Corollary:

A substitute becomes market uncompetitive when the provider fails to innovate with sufficient speed and creativity, gets greedy, or both.

Next, Distraction Theory.

Distraction Theory

Distraction Theory relies upon four assumptions:

1. Human attention is a finite commodity.[159] There are no known means of increasing the amount available beyond its natural limit.

2. Human attention has a range of optimal performance (maximum and minimum duration envelope) outside of which it cannot work effectively.

3. The number of tasks requiring attention has a roughly inverse square relationship to attention performance— *e.g.,* doubling the number of tasks ($X = 2$) reduces attention effectiveness to ¼ ($1/x^2$). *Multitasking* is so deleterious to mental performance that even *sitting next to someone who is multitasking* has been found to degrade attention and processing.[160]

4. Attention is engaged, disturbed, and redirected more efficiently by emotions than by either logic or facts.[161]

Distraction Theory is used in almost every marketing and propaganda technique in vogue. Other methods exist, but they are both more complicated to deploy and narrower in their effect. Sex sells, so does prestige, so does a sense of belonging. But what a teenybopper considers a tasteful display of flesh, the Fixodent-black-coffee-and-fiber-laxative klatch may well find grotesquely immodest. And what the elders find to be tastefully suggestive, is likely to consider granny-underpants boring to their *Alien-Sex-Fiend*-loving[162] youths.[163] The urbanite's sleek

Italian dream of a sportscar suggests a certain delicacy[164] (meaning *questionable sexuality*) to the country boy, and the lifted F-250 of the *Proud 'Murican* is a road-hogging abomination to the Perrier drinker in the skinny suit.

But distraction is universal.

Scream in someone's ear, beat their door with a hammer, drop their bone china on the floor and take a pratfall—your target may not know what you are saying or *why*, but his train of thought will derail nonetheless, be the rails standard-gauge, Russian-gauge, Bosnian-gauge, or the not-quite-interoperable-with-anything-else-gauge used by the Hong Kong MTR.

Social media is the closest that exists to a system built exclusively on Distraction Theory.[165] The actual content is singularly irrelevant—it is not designed to be processed with any sophistication, nor is it likely to be in front of the viewer long enough to make a distinct impression—so long as it effectively draws the target's attention from somewhere else, it has done its job.[166]

And the more social media evolves, the more dependent on Distraction Theory it becomes. *Myspace*—a music site turned social media site turned music platform (again)—was too song-centered and too inconsistent in design from one screen to the next to engender the mindless page hopping and petty arguments of *Facebook*. Facebook relied too much on long messages to encourage the hate scrolling and shoot-from-the-hip responses of *Twitter*.[167] Twitter required reading, and thus some token level of cognitive processing relative to *TikTok*. TikTok, being a video site, requires use of the visual cortex. Presumably, the next social media platform will use direct-to-the-limbic-system wiring to effectuate flashes of pure *feels*—finely tuned and corporate-controlled focal seizures.[168]

78

The goal of this technology is simple—to incentivize attentional shifts in such rapid succession that higher intellectual operations remain either perpetually nascent— never growing past the stage of shrieking and shit-excreting, or better yet, are aborted before they are much more than zygotes, unattached to the blood-rich walls of a fertile mind.

This is "Harrison Bergeron" with a twist—the handicap radios are purely voluntary, and the line for them stretches to the most remote reaches of the internet.[169]

Distraction Theory can be applied to one of two major ends—either the inhibition of movement (overload paralysis) or the induction of malleability (causing the target to become so overwhelmed that the decision-making process is handed over to another party or to the subconscious). Properly implemented, techniques based on Distraction Theory can induce one state as easily as another, or both states in quick succession. Either way, the individual will is rendered inert and replaced with inchoate excitement and the direction of the distraction makers—*the propagandists*.

The most widespread application of Distraction Theory is simple but economically critical in a consumer society—that of encouraging impulse purchases of things the targets do not need, do not want (except for during the most transient of moments), and cannot very well afford.[170] But one should not underestimate Distraction Theory's remarkable utility based on this pedestrian application.

Distraction Theory would seem to overlap with Substitution Theory, and in certain domains, it may. Our willful *Bergeron-ization* relies upon both, with Substitution Theory being what gives electronic media much of its appeal (by providing lower-cost substitutes to older forms of interaction and entertainment) and Distraction Theory underpinning its ability to produce a captive population that has more monkey-brain emotions than well-ordered thoughts.

Thus concludes our theoretical preparation. In the next section, we consider the application of what we have learned.

Application of Theories to Circumvent Thucydides's Trap

The goal of this text—to provide a plan of action and source of inspiration to those who wish to prevent America from falling into Thucydides's Trap—and its relationship to the theories thus covered should not be difficult to surmise. Positional Insecurity Theory, Substitution Theory, and Distraction Theory all provide powerful means to manipulate human behavior. By correctly harnessing them, we—the responsible citizens—should be able to prevent the national elite from initiating a global conflagration to end all conflagrations. This will not be easy, but it will likely challenge and engage. Here is what to do:

1. We must promote the right sort of infighting to keep the national elite at each other throats until Thucydides's Trap is well behind us.[171] (*Positional Insecurity Theory*)

2. We must identify what the national elite want and hold most dear and develop practical substitutes to quench whatever thirsts they have in such a way that their lust for power will either be extinguished or overcome by other lusts of greater ferocity. Ideally, these substitutes will also be shockingly addictive, at least on a psychological level, so that we may retain power over them for a longer time.[172] (*Substitution Theory*)

3. We must *distract, distract, distract!* Coherent thought on the part of the national elite must become impossible. (*Distraction Theory*)

A good tactic is not likely to be rest upon a single theory, but most will rely more upon one theory than another.

Advice, Admonishment, and Encouragement

The tactics suggested throughout this section are not meant to be all-inclusive. Rather, they are a starting point—a few ideas for the dedicated and capable American to use for preliminary action. Readers should apply the full force of their creativity. Their ideas are likely to be superior to anything contained herein. And the greater number and range of novel tactics are applied to control the destructive potential of the national elite, the more difficult developing psychological, cultural, or economic countermeasures is likely to be. The only admonishment I offer is this: Keep your actions within the bounds of the law. You will do America, yourself, and the world no good if you are sitting in prison.

Positional Insecurity Theory—Essential Tactics

These are but a few of many possible Positional Insecurity Theory tactics. Build upon them to your heart's and spirit's content.

PIT Tactic 1: Promote Overproduced Elites (only the angry ones) to Positions of Power

Fire with fire is time-tested and easily understood. The only question is *with what do you set the blaze and where do you start it?* In the context of Positional Insecurity Theory, an easy application of this is to promote vengeful overproduced elites to positions of maximum retribution. *What are the requirements for ideal (for our purposes) overproduced elites?*

1. They must have gone to the right schools—meaning a member of the Ivy League. A few West Coast school (Stanford) graduates might also be included on the list, but

no one who completed their degree at a school in flyover country should be considered. (This restriction is a matter of prestige, not quality of education.)

2. They must have an intense hatred for the institutions and people who failed to recognize their (self-identified) greatness. Whatever disdain they have for the commoners must be entirely overpowered by a fury born of rejection.

3. They must have less interest in reforming the elite gatekeeping systems than in vaporizing them.

4. They must *not* be suicidal.

5. They must have charm, charisma, and the ability to engage an audience.

6. They must be reasonably intelligent (*not a given*, regardless of prestigious credentials).

The three most obvious positions from which these people may wreak havoc on the established national elite are *1) elected official, 2) political advisor,* or *3) media personality.*

The odds that one will personally encounter a member of the (high-ranking) overproduced elite are not high, but nor are they miniscule, and they can be improved. With the right search parameters, dedication, and a bit of legwork one should be able to find a few candidates in even a city of modest size.

Such candidates are likely to be discontentedly, desperately grasping the lower or middle rungs of government or education or affiliated with a non-profit organization. *Non-profits* seem to be a particularly likely place for overproduced elites to hide from the harshness of the villeins' world while still maintaining some small shred of dignity. And candidates are more likely to be in smaller, newer cities than in old, established ones, where they might be recognized by their more successful peers.

As for cultivating these people—such is likely to require great care. The useful ones are not stupid. And they may well detect attempts at deception. Thus, honesty is likely the best policy. If you can befriend one of these people, such is best done by expressing what must serve as a shared belief—*that the national elites are dangerous and incompetent and that actions must be taken to stop them.*

Rather than micromanaging these people, one should collaborate with them towards a common goal, recognizing both their and your unique talents.

The most critical apparatus for ensuring that one is not duped into helping an overproduced elite get into a position of power and then being discarded by said elite is *intuition*. The overproduced elites you promote must *not* see themselves as *equal to* the established elites, but *better than them*. The overproduced elites must have *contempt* for those they would replace. Love, hate, fear, and anger can all be transformed and diminished over time, but contempt is durable.[173] Contempt is a pound of garlic being dumped into a two-gallon kettle of soup: Other fragrances may well be there, but they will remain forever overpowered.

PIT Tactic 2: Encourage Intragroup Attacks Amongst the Established Elites

The average American has little say in policy, but he can at least pick a fight online. And this can be enough. Intragroup conflict amongst the established elite is on the upswing. Such is why the members of the United States Congress are increasingly likely to publicly ridicule each other,[174] consider censuring their peers,[175] and push to expel those they believe have crossed a line.[176] This is good, and this is something upon which we can capitalize.

We have seen senators run from office on the flimsiest of #MeToo accusations. And there is nothing unbiased about #MeToo, with certain weak claims taken seriously,[177] and more serious claims ignored,[178] establishing that #MeToo is just another political tool. With a bit of pushing, these intragroup attacks (be they centered on sex or something else) can be made more common. All we need to remember is that elected officials are at least nominally human, and most of them are online. With a bit of nudging, any number of them can be steered towards embarrassing themselves or wrecking their careers with a misworded, impulsively written Tweet.[179]

In theory, the members of the national elite could spurn social media altogether, and some will; however, such is not an entirely feasible option for most elected officials. They *need* some online presence, and they *want* some online presence. Bear in mind that D.C. is *Hollywood for Ugly People*—one rarely goes into politics without some desire for attention.[180]

Social media does not favor all voices equally. It is optimized for the most active and the most strident—those who are willing to dedicate themselves to a cause or ideology in a manner ordinary people would not or could not—those who are adept at identifying people in need of identity and engaging in the laborious work of cultivating them.[181] Thus, fanatics are favored. They can immerse themselves fully in their beliefs more easily than can most (they oftentimes have nothing else). And their sheer persistence demands that they be heard. This ability to scream above the noise gives them outsized effects on political policy, thus leading to greater political segregation and a more vindictive style of engagement.

We can support infighting amongst the national elite by engaging with the radicals, not in a way that would lead to criminal charges, but by supporting their positions and amplifying them on social media to the extent that we can legally do so. We can also develop and promote absurd and ever-changing ideologically influenced standards of behavior,[182] piling vitriol on any member of the national elite who fails to perfectly conform to impossible to understand and impractical to implement standards of language usage,[183] doctrinal purity, and personal conduct.[184] The idea behind all of this is to force the established national elites into a Sisyphean game of defense. The more time they spend fending off attacks on their coveted roles, the less time they will have to develop grand strategies to restore the empire.

Positional Insecurity Theory—Final Thoughts

Despite their hubris, even the most egomaniacal of the elite know this: *Sic transit gloria mundi*—thus passes worldly glory. They know that power can be taken from them. They may deny it, they may pretend that they are the exception, but somewhere in the darkest reaches of their psyche is the guillotine, the noose, or the cellar of the Ipatiev House.[185] Even those with the greatest of certitude in the peaceful transition of power fear banishment to the hinterlands—knowing that *without their connections* few of them could do much more than *adjunct-ing* their way from one cow college contract to the next or selling used cars in Tuscaloosa. This they may well dread above all else: being stuck somewhere so awful they will be able to *sense* from blocks away the stink of supercenter detergent, canned beer, and vo-tech graduates and where the only way to get a decent ribeye is by overnight delivery.[186]

Many of them might well prefer Bolsheviks with pistols and bayonets—at least there is some small romantic dignity in death at the hands of reprobates (aside from one's children being *shot, bludgeoned, stabbed, and shot again*).[187] But to the national elite, there is none in teaching remedial poly-sci to partially rehabilitated ex-cons who work seven nights a week at the poultry processing plant as part of their court-ordered drug rehabilitation and who complete their assignments using the county library's Wi-Fi.[188]

Positional Insecurity Theory is a powerful tool. It attacks the very core of the national elite's identity, but alone it is not enough. If allowed time to regroup and restructure their thoughts, the elites will develop countermeasures to positional attacks. We must never give them time enough to think. Thus, we turn to Distraction Theory and its applications.

Distraction Theory—Essential Tactics

DT Tactic 1: Promote Lunatics and Artists as Generators of Unusual Thought

There is nothing more disruptive to the operation of complex organizational systems than the unknown and unforeseeable. It grinds smooth the gears of pencil-pushing organizations and their automatons. Given that our targets— the established elite—derive their power from bureaucracies, this is worth bearing in mind. And it is one of the reasons that artists can prove so shockingly destructive when they gain dominion over a system (with another reason being what we shall consider below).

Adolf Hitler painted[189] and had a strong appreciation for design, so much so that kept an architect (Albert Speer) in his inner circle.[190] Vladimir Lenin wrote extensively.[191] Mao Zedong was a calligrapher, poet,[192] and writer.[193] His most famous wife (Madame Mao) was an actress[194] who wrote and directed operas.[195] Joseph Stalin was a poet.[196] And Idi Ami played the accordion[197] (in addition to being *His Excellency, President for Life, Field Marshal Al Hadji Doctor Idi Amin Dada, VC, DSO, MC, CBE, Lord of All the Beasts of the Earth and Fishes of the Seas and Conqueror of the British Empire in Africa in General and Uganda in Particular*— according to his self-awarded, *creatively* immodest title).[198]

None of these people were virtuosos in the conventional arts, but that is not to say they lacked creative ambition. They had enough inventive ability and conceit to imbue them with both grand visions and a willingness to annihilate—to paint over old canvas, to chip away at the imperfections in the stone. In any artist of real competence, there is a certain supernal cruelty—a willingness to slaughter and abandon their misbegotten creations—with the greatest difference between the dictator and the writer or painter being that the latter two have a page or watercolor board upon which they may execute their ideas, the former, an entire nation.

And in dictators, a little creativity goes a long way.

The great strength—and weakness—of creatives is that they cannot think as other people do.[199] And this makes responding to them and their mental gyrations in a timely manner difficult, for the pathologically rigid most of all. Likewise, moderated insanity proves equally confounding. Sorting the ideas of the creative and the insane takes time— they do not fit conveniently into boxes.

Creativity and insanity are not the same, although there is limited evidence they correlate.[200] Nevertheless, from the perspective of the rigid system and the entrenched members of such systems, they both pose a similar threat in that they introduce unpredictability. Unpredictability leads to delays, and that is enough for our purposes.

The goal of all of this is to *distract*—to draw the attention of the organization and its member—so that their attention is too divided for them to engage in the tasks assigned to them.

At the legislative and executive level, this application is easy—promote and vote for political candidates who are unpredictable enough to confound and persistent enough to make ignoring them impossible. Only be mindful of giving artists—disgruntled artists most of all—too much power, on the chance that their grand vision can only be built upon a tower of skulls. And be certain to compliment their creations and performances *before* they are handed the reins of government. This reads as being more authentic than praise given after the fact, and doing so just may save you a (decoratively placed) bullet to the heart.

At the entrenched bureaucratic level, installing creative and otherwise unpredictable people gets considerably harder. Bureaucracies are adept at selecting for predictability.[201] (They must be. Their survival depends on as much.) But that is not to say such is impossible. One needs to but apply the proper tool to the task.

Understanding Diversity, Weaponizing Diversity

For this section, diversity shall be categorized as being one of two types. The first, *conventional diversity*, entails exactly what one imagines diversity entails—diversity of skin color, hair type, religion, and sexual orientation.[202] It *does not* entail a more substantial diversity of thoughts or modes of information processing. Practically, it can be antithetical to as much, as institutions may emphasize more rigidly conventional thinking even as they grow to appear more varied—*looks different, thinks the same.*

The second category of diversity is *mindset, perspective, and thought diversity*. Promoting this category of diversity *may* entail hiring people from different ethnic, religious, or cultural backgrounds, but it may not. Two white men (or two black women or whatever demographic one prefers) may well have nearly identical life perspectives and approaches to problem-solving, but such is not guaranteed. The same could be said for highly diverse sets of people. One selecting for *thought diversity* should examine both the problem-solving and information-processing approaches of the people involved, not their physical traits.[203]

Conventional diversity is a limited threat to the power structure of the elites. It may reduce cohesion and understanding and produce a more distant and detached work culture, but it does not inevitably affect the operation of the elite's systems. Even thought diversity is only disruptive to *most* of the power structure, with some small parts of that structure being able to tolerate it and (occasionally) put it to good use.

In theory, thought and perspective diversity *could* improve the overall efficiency and operation of organizations. The mentally unique could spot weaknesses in procedures and systems that others might well miss and devise novel solutions the conventional would be hard-pressed to create. Those advocating aggressively for a broader model of diversity can make this argument loudly, truthfully, and without reservation. This *should* work, and government and large corporate interests should be the better for it.

In practice, it will not. There are only a few highly autonomous parts of the elite power structure that can channel unusual and creative thinking into increased power and stability—many of them in (or affiliated with) the military.

DARPA, with its long history of innovation, stands out as one of the best examples.[204] And several brave leaders within the power structure of the armed forces have proven dedicated to thinking outside the box—Albert Stubblebine,[205] who played an instrumental role in the United States Army's psychic research (*Stargate Project*) certainly demonstrated a willingness to consider unconventional technologies, although his career suffered for it.[206]

A review of some of the more offbeat programs that have existed within government suggests that the military may be *more* flexible and open to novel ideas than the civilian sector. From Project Iceworm (a plan to hide nuclear missiles under ice caps in Greenland)[207] to the Edgewood Arsenal human experiments (in which many psychoactive substances were tested on soldiers)[208] to a project overseen by behaviorist B.F. Skinner to develop pigeon-guided missiles,[209] the military has imagined and funded many new and unusual ways to turn live enemies into dead ones.

The exact reason that the military seems to better tolerate eccentric problem-solvers is impossible to determine without an investigation beyond the scope of this text, and there appear to be few published studies on the matter. One possibility is that militaries, more than civilian agencies, *must* demonstrate some flexibility—war is inherently unpredictable and the stakes at play are enormous.[210] *From great competition and struggle often comes great innovation.*[211]

They may also be more adept at adapting to unusual thinking *due to* (rather than *despite*) their unambiguous chain of command. Once rules are well-defined and authority is delineated, a certain latitude of conduct can be tolerated. Someone *is* in charge of a certain activity or group of individuals, and the person in charge can rest assured that he or she can give orders, design projects, receive credit, and accept blame within that domain. In a system where authority is hopelessly diffuse and uncertainly apportioned, the natural result is paralysis—no one does anything even slightly risky due to power and responsibility falling upon many people in general and no one in particular. This *uncertain-power paralysis* accounts for much of the inertia in academia (and tremendous reliance on committees—where everyone has *a say*, but no one has the *final* say).[212]

Thus, in keeping in line with our intent to prevent the national elite from tossing us genitals first into Thucydides's Trap, creative people—the *authentically diverse*—should not be encouraged to join the armed forces. The military is likely to either put them to some practical use or, if they are too unruly in their behavior, discharge them in short order.

Creativity and diversity are not the enemies of military command and discipline—*ideology* is. The more politically (rather than *mission*) directed a military becomes, the less likely it is to be able to effectively execute its mission. Constant fear of removal based on politics is uncomfortable and demoralizing for those who are not political cadres or political officers—which populated the People's Liberation Army and the Red Army in considerable numbers.[213] Demoralization and career uncertainty also undermine command authority. When commanders know that one ill-phrased comment or any apparent lack of enthusiasm for political purges and programs can be used against them by those who either *want* their job or who simply want *someone else* to have their jobs (as might a displeased subordinate), they will spend less time leading and more time guarding their careers and ass(ets).[214]

And the truly political animal favored by an ideologically managed army is of a dissimilar sort from those likely to lead a nation to victory. There is a reason that excellent wartime leaders—Winston Churchill for one—make for mediocre peacetime ones.[215] The skillset required is different.

There is some evidence that the higher ranks of the armed forces contain at least a few careerists more adept at playing politics than at winning war games.[216] Political careerists, regardless of whatever conventionally diverse traits they possess, want something *very different* from what a true leader wants. A good and dedicated leader *wants authority* and is willing to *accept responsibility*. A careerist wants *opportunity* (for advancement) and needs *deniability*. Plant enough careerists in any organization, but it an armed one or otherwise, and it will start to look quite a bit like academia—where the closest one encounters to fighting is *cover-your-rear combat*—fascinating to watch, if only because almost all the armor worn by the participants is strapped to their backsides.

Lunatics: Considerations and Cautions

Finally, there is the matter of promoting the truly mentally unwell or unstable to positions of power. This should be done with some care, if for no other reason than it, if poorly executed, stands to be quite cruel to the unwell person so promoted. Depressives, paranoids, and the deeply fearful *should not* be subjected to needless derision and attack. Rather, the only lunatics who should be kicked up the political stairs are those who would stand to enjoy the process and not be harmed by it. As for who should be promoted—this is a judgment call. *If we promote this person, will he have fun, and will he remain relatively unscathed by the experience?* If you can answer *yes* to both questions, go ahead and start a *Loony Tunes for Senate* campaign. If answering *no* to either question, proceed only at your moral hazard.

Next, sex.

DT Tactic 2: Sexualizing Everything

There are few greater distractors than sex.[217] Dreams of decadent cheesecakes, juicy cuts of meat, delectable vegetables, and fabulous fruit may occupy hours of one's time. But there are limits. Once the man distracted by the delicatessen is properly fed, his thoughts move to other things, at least for some time. The appetite for sex; however, is never really sated, partially because it is a complex desire, one associated with status, standards of beauty, and sense of self-worth. The other reason: There is a limited supply of even marginally decent sex, whereas palatable food is a commodity available to almost anyone, save the very poorest. Thus, there is a *sex scarcity* to a greater extent than there is a food scarcity (at least in the developed world, although the opposite might well be the case in the developing world). There have been a range of substitutes for sex invented, and these substitutes are of sufficient quality for them to effect a reduction in intrasexual male violence.[218] However, they are not quite perfect and leave at least a little something—as much a matter of perceived intimacy as physical stimulation—to be desired.

As robotics and artificial intelligence advance, sexual (and emotional intimacy) scarcity may be eradicated.[219] Such stands to render a non-negligible fraction of marketing techniques worthless and make most violent conflict impossible to sustain for anything longer than the participants find amusing. Until then, sexual images and messages remain one of the best approaches to derail an otherwise disciplined mind.

The application of the sexualization of everything can take several forms. First is the sex scandal. Sex scandals have been a part of American life since the days of Alexander Hamilton.[220] The modern difference—video and the internet. A cautionary note: One *absolutely should not* attempt to extort political leaders. This is a serious criminal offense. And extortion is not the point—destabilization of the political class is. Even without extortion, sex is a tool of great import.

Sexual Scandals and Political Churn

Most successful politicians are men[221] who are (at least nominally) straight, meaning that those best suited to engaging them in easily weaponized and career-kamikazeing affairs are women.[222] For those womenfolk who truly desire that the world be a more peaceful place, several possible courses of action come to mind. Not all demand a held nose and a *they-do-not-make-water-hot-enough-to-scald-away-the-filth* shower after the fact. For Anthony Weiner—a man so aptly named for the scandal that befell him that one must consider the possibility that the gods have been conspiring to despoil him since the moment of his conception, if not before—some virtual flirting and a few closeups of his gym shorts sent him down the road to perdition.[223] And in the age of #MeToo, even this much might not be required. Former Senator Al Franken was coerced into resigning because he *may* have touched a woman's buttocks a decade prior to the accusation against him being leveled and because he *held his hands above a woman's breasts in a joking manner.*[224] In effect, he *telepathically violated her.*

This was enough to result in his banishment.

Men can also play a role in manipulating sexually undisciplined politicians. Consider *To Catch a Predator*—a show dedicated to what borders on entrapment of men who believe that they are communicating with underage girls (or boys). In truth, a similar approach can be taken without the use of anyone who is young or female. Some Youtubers do just that.[225]

Stock photos, convincing text chats—one should brush up on teenage popular culture before undertaking this—and voice-changing software can be used to produce a reasonably good digital simulacrum of a girl or woman. And developing technologies make the process of helping politicians to ruin themselves even easier. Consider the case of Yasuo Nakajima (@azusagakuyu), a middle-aged Japanese man with a love of motorcycles and a desire for an audience.[226] With a bit of photo editing and the use of a few filters, he managed to successfully present himself as a young, attractive female biker.[227] The application of these technologies for our purposes are obvious. Other advancing technologies, such as Deepfake image replacement, may also prove useful in coming years.[228] (Any person using these technologies should be mindful of the potential legal repercussions of using another's likeness, particularly without express permission.)

Tactics should be applied in such a way that neither side—left or right—is favored. Rather, the goal must be to promote *political churn*—the extraordinarily rapid installment and replacement of politicians—which is both damaging to any sense of community and camaraderie within the political system and is (more importantly) profoundly *distracting*.

Pearl Clutching as Offensive Tactic

Next, there is the matter of keeping the tenor of sexual and political discussion as shrilly Victorian as possible. Given that 89 percent of the world's pornographic content is produced in the United States,[229] a reasonable person might *reasonably* assume that a people none too easily offended by yards of writhing flesh and oil drums' worth of spraying bodily fluids would have a *continental* view of sex and sexual liaisons.[230] Alas, outside of law school textbooks, the *reasonable person* is a rare breed, and his mindset is shared by almost none.[231]

That we can go from pearl-clutching to pearl-necklace making in a matter of minutes is both fascinating and terrifying—boundless hypocrisy makes for much cognitive dissonance and subsequent frustration, confusion, and volatility of conduct.

The pharisees' words are sharp, double-edged swords and easily wielded against their owners. And let us make no mistake about it, there are pharisees amongst us, and they are more fecal-stained outhouse seats than *whited sepulchers*.[232] They and their duplicitousness are devices well made to our—the responsible citizenry's—use.

Furthering the state of sexual panic is easy. And one may work from either the left or right perspectives.

If intending to work from the left, one only needs to join any radical feminist or radical feminist-ally group and promote the most puritanical and moralistic hogwash yet to be devised by humankind. The key to making this work: Focus on power imbalances and sexual inequality.

Andrea Dworkin—a mentally disturbed and sex-phobic feminist—laid out the theory quite well.[233] Although Dworkin never said that "all sex is rape," she did state that "Under patriarchy, every woman's son is her betrayer and also the inevitable rapist or exploiter of another woman."[234] And this reflects an interesting notion: Until the *alleged* power imbalance between the sexes is eliminated, heterosexual coitus and almost all other intersexual interaction remain acts of domination ("Whatever intercourse is, it is not freedom . . . "). And women who consent to sex within a patriarchal society are *collaborating* with the patriarchy and hurting womankind ("Instead occupied women [women engaging in vaginal sex while living in a patriarchal society] will be collaborators, more base in their collaboration than other collaborators have ever been: experiencing pleasure in their own inferiority . . . ").[235]

Said another way: So long as there is *any* remnant of male privilege (defined in the broadest terms), no heterosexual coitus can be fully consensual and non-exploitative.

To understand how absurd this is, one should apply the foundation of her theory—the notion that only agreements between perfect equals are non-coercive—to any other part of law and social interaction. Consider transportation.

The average American retail worker makes slightly more than 29,000 USD per year.[236] For a worker in this position who wants to buy a new vehicle of even the most modest variety—a subcompact car, a motorcycle, or the like—financing or long-term saving are the routes most commonly available.[237] Even if said worker chooses something as decidedly undecadent as a Yamaha Zuma 125[238]—a barely highway-legal scooter with a maximum speed of 60 miles per hour[239]—the issue of money remains.

The most practical way to obtain financing for anything with two wheels is likely to be through vehicle dealer's approved financial services provider—in the case of someone wanting a Yamaha, Synchrony Finance,[240] a company that financed more than 140 billion USD of purchases in 2018.[241] And this apparent wealth affords the organization more than mere lending power. Synchrony Finance almost certainly has a stable of attorneys, collection agents, secretaries, and administrative staff that no ordinary worker could ever hope to employ. The point: By any reasonable measure, Synchrony Finance has more resources of every sort imaginable than does the average borrower. The two parties are *not* economically equal.

Nevertheless, we allow them to enter into a binding legal agreement—to consent to an arrangement founded on mutuality of consideration—and we hold the lesser party (the borrower) to the agreement, just as we do the greater one.[242] Granted, many consumer-protection laws restrict and shape the nature and terms of lending agreements.[243] But few, save perhaps actual communists, would suggest that consumer lending agreements are inherently unconscionable.

We tolerate some inequality of wealth, position, and power in contract law. Unless we are to seize and redistribute all personal and corporate resources (or ban contracts), we must.

And for those who consider this power differential to be beyond the pale, I invite you to consider government-backed student loans—borrowed primarily by young people (most having no resources of either the economic or experiential sort) from the United States government—arguably the most advantaged of parties—and under terms that make discharge of said debt in bankruptcy legendarily difficult.[244] If the pants-folding scooterist is at a disadvantage to Synchronicity, what is this? What is the student-borrower? Extremely disadvantaged? *Beyond unconscionably* disadvantaged?

Still, student loans continue to be disbursed, and few have advocated they be eliminated.

Dworkin's thinking is unhinged, impractical, and corrosive. It is also widespread in its application and has permeated education law[245] and family law[246] alike. More than anything else, it is tremendously useful.

Any relationship in which a man has power (and *all men* have power, we are told) over a woman—no matter how slight, ephemeral, or illusory—is shockingly coercive, profoundly abusive, and only a few steps removed from rape. Such conclusions stem more from an extension and expansion of Dworkin's thinking to every aspect of life than from her actual words. And such extremism quite effectively casts a pallor over even the most innocent of intersexual dynamics, making cooperation (or much interaction) all but impossible.[247]

And this is the space in which we live. The power of sexual panic has been evaluated—at least regarding #MeToo—but there is still more useful lunacy within the ore of today's disordered thinking to be mined and smelted. We may end up with as much slag as pig iron, but there is iron (and irony) aplenty.

Now that the left's pathological and contradictory sexual standards have been torn apart at length, the right should have its turn.

Christian sexual morality may be strict and inclined to make for some enduringly joyless marriages, but it is *not*, if kept within the biblical traditions, unsustainable, contradictory, or biased against either sex.[248] *Modern, chivalrous, and sexually liberated churchian beliefs* (and those elements *do* go together), however, are so wondrously contradictory that nary a soul, be it still attached to its corporeal form or wandering through eternity, could make any sense of them. The churches now happily fill their pews and pulpits with those who have broken their marriage vows for no other reason than boredom, mindbogglingly complex blended families, and syphilitic single mothers. What, if any, carnal practices are categorically forbidden within the modern church is difficult to ascertain.

There appears to be considerable resistance to accepting practicing (and admitted) homosexuals into most churches, although this is changing. [249] Perhaps recognition of the transgendered is not far behind. Pornography is formally frowned upon (despite a decent number of professed Christians watching it)[250]—because it is apparently considered closer to adultery than serial matrimony, despite *Jesus himself* making clear that the married, divorced, and remarried are not to be considered married at all. [251] Presumably, child molestation and bestiality are beyond the pale. But those are not much accepted by even the most *freak-flag-flying* sexual liberationists. There appears much anxiety about sex on the right, but it is the nonspecific anxiety of those who know only *that* they fear, but not *what* or *why*.

In truth, both the fringe left and the hard conservative right have similar views on sex. They simply are not aware of as much.

Here is what they have in common:

1. *They both oppose pleasure.* Left or right, ideologues are killjoys. If they knew how to enjoy life, they would not be ideologues. Dworkin was terrified of men's sexuality (however unlikely it was that she was on the receiving end of it).[252] The extreme religious right is equally terrified of its own (male) sexuality.[253] *Penises are scary.* And god or goddesses forbid that anyone *enjoy* a sexual encounter. Sex must be either political act[254] or religious act. Those who are no more enthusiastic about their liaisons turning into (brief!) horizontal recitations of *Das Kapital* than

they are about having unions drier than a communion cracker are out of luck.[255]

2. *They are confused.* Neither the radical left nor the radical right have any substantial sense of sexual morality. They have *vague* ideas of a romanticized world in which sex is something *wonderful? Fantastic? Awe-inspiring? Godly? Liberating? Transcendent?* They do not know what sex should be, only that it should be something more than it is, despite *what it is*—an act of reproduction, entertainment, profit, or some combination thereof—being all it can be.

3. *They want to stand for something, preferably more than chivalry or hate, but they simply do not know what.* And this is the most important point: *They dream of having a dream. They hope for hope. They aspire to aspire.* This lack of certainty makes them tremendously vulnerable to attack.

4. *They are both deeply sexually frustrated and likely to see even the most innocent encounters in a perverse light.* Yet their perceptions are counter to reality. It is not difficult for the average man or woman to go through weeks of life without seeing much worthy of sexual note. And there is a reason most of us have never considered careers in adult entertainment: We know that no one would pay to see us naked.

So similar are the two sides in their pathologies and paranoias that the techniques to manipulate them are identical: All the citizenry must do is infiltrate these movements and promote the most deranged voices and irrational moments of panic to the fore. These people—the estrogen-toxic left and the Bible-thumping right are *loud*. They make noise enough to drown out almost everything else.

101

And that makes them distracting.

The more fires these useful idiots are encouraged to set, the more time the national elite must spend putting them out. Congressional hearings on *satanic dog molestation*—that is easily worth six months of impassioned speeches in the House of Representatives. *Breath rape* (when a man exhales too heavily within earshot of a woman, I suppose)—the Senate Armed Services, Budget, and Finance Committees *must* hold special 14-hour-a-day hearings on the matter. Overly lifelike illustrations of frog genitalia in middle-school textbooks—who could object to a blue-ribbon presidential commission on that?

The responsible citizen should turn these forces of destruction into something good—a foil against the vicious tendencies of the elite. And there is poetry in this—the out of control, the peripheral, and the paranoid can draw power from the controllers, the established, and the fearless to make the world a bit better.

The Impossibility of Satire

No matter how extreme, how unhinged, or how detached from reality a position or argument is, some community of fanatics will accept it if given time and a bit of prodding, so long as the argument is made with a straight face.

Pure reactionaries, regardless of nominally leftist or rightist identities, are fundamentally unmoored. And that lack of absolute values and core beliefs, aside from disgust and frustration, makes them gullible. For extremists, there is no satire (and little humor). And a society dominated by them becomes humorless as well.[256] Dedicated citizens who wish to weaponize the institutions and ideologies of the sexually insecure—radical and academic feminist or purity-pledge ultra-right—must only remember that *one cannot go too far!* The infiltrator must have no shame. No matter how absurdly repressive the solution offered, there is a real possibility that the extremists will seriously consider it. Even if they dismiss the idea as unworkable, they are likely to admire the infiltrator's passion.

Knowing this and acting accordingly, one is nearly bound to succeed.

Sex (and Sexlessness) Sells

America is past the age of peak sexually suggestive advertisements.[257] A few companies push against boundaries (or *transgress them* if you will) well into the realm of hypersexuality, but those companies are at the margins, courting controversy.[258] The rest are quickly being shamed and harangued into body positivity,[259] fat acceptance, and squeaky-clean Virgin-Mary innocence.[260]

Plenty of female social media stars are willing to allow the male gaze to exploit them (for a fee),[261] and adult entertainers (or at least some former ones) are quickly becoming household names.[262] Blunt discussions of sexual orientation, sexual techniques, and transgenderism are so common as to barely warrant the batting of an eye: We are not entirely sexless, at least in our thoughts and discourse.[263]

Instead, this reflects a peculiar bifurcation in our society—sex can be either pornographically and anatomically explicit or entirely nonexistent from a conversation, but there is no acceptable middle. This was not the state of cultural affairs even ten years ago. Such is at least partially the result of the actions of the extremist groups (left and right) already considered. Their techniques—consumer boycotts and social media attacks—work *some* of the time on *some* organizations, but only if the organizations are concerned with *family-friendly* appeal. They can easily cudgel Calvin Klein into swearing off ever producing another advertisement like those it made with Brooke Shields and Kate Moss, but Calvin Klein needs available-at-the-mall acceptance. Eckhaus Latta does not.[264]

The victims of this purge—suggestiveness, nuance, and implicitness—were not long mourned nor may they be much missed. They were quiet voices, easily muted by the orgiastic moans of hedonists and the *praise-Jesus-and-pass-the-blame-and-all-sex-is-more-or-less-rape-anyway* unified shrieking of the radical left/radical right *porn-war* alliance.[265] Still, the victims had their uses. And a language where all is denotation and nothing is connotation is legalistic at best and algorithmic at worst.

This is the principal effect of extremism run rampant: It is less likely to eliminate serious threats to its underlying beliefs than it is to hollow out of the middle. Dialogues become contract negotiations, elections become *battles royale*,[266] and speeches, *either-you-are-with-us-or-with-the-terrorists* prayer calls for loyalty.[267]

Specific to the domain of sex and sexlessness, the current environment offers us a *perversely* powerful tool against the national elite. All we must do is earnestly make a few schizoid and contradictory demands. They are:

1. We must require that our leaders be sexless on command, have no impure thoughts about their colleagues or subordinates, and are so devoted to their spouses that even a crack team of relationship counselors can find no fault.[268]

104

2. We must demand that they show no signs of prudishness or sanctimony and that they are accepting of a laundry list of sexual practices and perspectives of length and complexity sufficient to have driven Freud to overdose on cocaine.[269]

3. We must stress that they demonstrate appropriate respect for the *decadence du jour* while taking a firm stand against perversion, which we must be certain to define in only the vaguest know-it-when-I-see-it manner (if we choose to define it at all).[270]

4. We must alternate between feigning autism-spectrum literalness and octogenarian church-lady sensitivity to language. When a politician (or any other member of the national elite) *wants* to imply something sexual, we must pretend to be so entirely unsubtle that we take a prolonged metaphor of a red-tipped rocket repeatedly crashing into the icy surface of Uranus as a fascinating recounting of an obscure NASA mission. But when hearing statements made in perfect innocence, we must affect such sensitivity that even the most innocuously technical description of inserting a male plug into a female socket sends us to the fainting couch.[271]

Not many politicians can fully comply with these requirements. Some manage to break the rules and charm their way out of disabling sanction and criminal prosecution (Bill Clinton).[272] A very few manage to ignore them altogether, with Donald Trump being the most obvious example. But Trump is not so much a politician as he is a wrecking ball with a spray tan and improbable hair.[273] He is, despite his wealth and status, an outsider elite. And the wondrous power of an angry member of the outsider/overproduced elite is something we have considered at length.

For the rest of the national elite, navigating this terrain is an endless distraction. And distractions are what will keep the national elite too busy to execute any grand and grandly harmful plans.

Next, we apply the extremists' effect—that of making the middle ground impossible—to the broader realm of non-sexual politics by way of Substitution Theory.

Substitution Theory—Essential Tactics

The line between distraction and substitution can be thin (if it exists at all). Distractions monopolize time and mental energy. They *substitute* unproductive effort for its more meaningful sibling. And substitutions *distract* from primary goals. Still, there is a functional difference between the two within this text.

A *distraction* consumes time but makes no convincing claim to be equal to the thing it replaces. Interference built upon Distraction Theory is obvious to its targets, who know (or will surmise in short order) that their time is being consumed by efforts they find less than enjoyable or optimally productive.

A substitution *entices* its targets by way of offering something that satisfies an urge or longing for less time, money, or energy than can be had by the original means the substitution supplants. Interference built upon Substitution Theory may never be obvious to its targets, and even targets who eventually determine that they have been subject to manipulation may be so pleased with the substitution that they choose to continue their reliance upon it.

And this is where the extremists' bimodal effect on public discourse becomes both fascinating and useful. Well applied, it allows for the genuine consensus-based accomplishment to be replaced with a more viscerally satisfying zero-sum game approach to politics.[274] And this is just the sort of *substitution* needed to keep the national elite from forming cogent plans to remake the world in their image or protect themselves from external threats to power.

ST Tactic 1: Facilitating Endless Arguments: Replacing Real Achievement with Token Victories

The beauty of social media is that it amplifies the id in a manner that is instantaneous, non-destructive to cognitive processes, immediately reversible, profoundly addictive, and often undetectable to its users. It *begs* for an immediate response.[275] It *cries out* to crush thought and reason and replace them with the emanations of the heart, the gut, and the groin. And it promotes bickering, territorialism, tribalism, and misunderstanding more efficiently than any previous form of communication. The other great effect: Its norms of neonate impulsivity and endless bellicosity are spilling out and into the realm of politics.[276] Only the most tenacious or thickheaded believe that much persuasion and progress can derive from a Twitter deathmatch. Still, they engage people both rich and poor, educated and ignorant alike.

As this style of debate spreads, less gets done. If we—the responsible Americans—wish to see that the national elite do as little (harmful or otherwise) as possible, we need only to rope them to the Twitter melee and drag them down to the lowest level.

Intelligent and levelheaded people could easily resist this— their disciplined minds could spot the pitfall we have dug and walk around it. Fortunately for us, this is not likely. The national elite have been almost entirely insulated from reproach for much of their lives. They may be happy to heap smugness on others—those of the wrong class or background[277]—but being on the receiving end of mockery of their incompetence is bound to be an incongruous and horrifying experience for them.[278] Resisting the urge to *fight back* against the ungrateful masses will prove nearly impossible.

But the elite's record of winning virtual barroom brawls is not great. Thus, they are going to great lengths to block, ban, and shut down any criticism that threatens their credibility and authority.[279] This applies to social media. It also applies to the comment sections of major websites and newspapers.

Our lords and masters do not take criticism well.

This poses an obstacle, but not an insurmountable one. The most apparent approach to escaping the choking clutches of the powers that be is to platform hop—to move from one social media outlet to the next—or to create a platform of one's own. Another is to develop and use algorithm-confusing codespeak and a robust symbolism (drawn from popular imagery, films, etc.) as a multimedia argot.[280] An additional one is to constantly change avatars and topics. A final method is to *adopt a conventional argument that is aligned with the alleged belief of the target elite and accuse the elite of violating some tenant of it.*

This is not so much about finding a controversial position as it is about finding the spot of sin and impurity on the target. Saul Alinsky advocated a similar approach—that of *make the enemy live up to its own book of rules.*[281] The difference I advocate is that you specifically present yourself as a *concerned friend and ally* who firmly believes those rules. This sort of infiltration aligns with the methods described in *Pearl Clutching as Offensive Tactic*, but the difference between the present method and the former is that the present may have no connection to sex. It also bears some relation to the methods described in *Encourage Intragroup Attacks Amongst the Established Elites*, but that is restricted to *intragroup* hostility, whereas this is a broader approach that encourages fights with *anyone, anywhere, over any topic*. And Positional Insecurity Theory tactics are based on fear. Substitution Theory tactics, with few exceptions, are not.

There are two keys to this tactic. The first is to remember that the topic is irrelevant. The topic is a pretext to draw in the elite, to get them to join in a messy fight in the messiest way possible. Pretend friendship, pretend loyalty, pretend anything necessary to engage them in a ruckus. And if the national elite prove unwilling to battle you online, start an argument on their behalf against their opposition, and plead for their assistance.

The second is this: *Be entertaining*. Never underestimate the ability to engage people with a snappy comeback, a rapier wit, or a perfectly landed insult. This key is more important than the first. *Engage* the elite. Make them *want* to argue with you (or someone else). Make the crowd cheer, boo, scream, or gasp as loudly as possible. The goal is not to *win* the fight. The goal is to keep the other side fighting. And if you do win, do not win too hard or too often. A conflict where the winner is certain is not worth watching. If you are the better fighter, toy with your opponent. This consumes his time, makes him angrier, and invites careless moves from him—redirect his energy and his ego.[282] Use them against him.

The other thing to do—cheerlead. People like to be noticed. They like being liked. Monitor the feeds and pages of the prominent national elite and boost the most controversial messages and arguments they make. In doing so, you provide an incentive, however small, for your target to self-radicalize, to bicker with his peers. Even the most elite of the elite love an adoring audience. Many are uniquely vulnerable to the intoxication of one because they have come to expect admiration. They feel underappreciated and confused without it.

ST Tactic 2: Sell the Elites Bullshit. Convince Them of Its Greatness. Laugh All the Way to the Bank

Introduction

This section is the second to present arts and artists as weapons against the elite. A previous section—*Promote Lunatics and Artists as Generators of Unusual Thought*—considers the opacity of the artist's mind as a tool for the ensnarement and perplexment of the elites. This section considers the power of the arts themselves.

Caveat

This section contains a protocol that is the most difficult to execute promptly of any within the text. I have included it as much to provoke thought as for anything else. Building up a reputation as an artist oftentimes takes *years*, and that is time the world does not have if Thucydides's Trap is not to catch us all. Perhaps more industrious people can take what I have written and apply it to social media or some other emerging forum to engage and distract the elites.

To the young and young at heart who read this: I do not doubt your competence in the realms of social engineering and high technology. Little would make me happier than to see your ideas and methods eclipse my own. Above all else, never hesitate *to be a bastard*.[283]

And enjoy it!

Fashion Over Beauty

Creating art, regardless of form or era—art in the highest and most developed sense of the works of Dürer,[284] Fellini,[285] Hokusai,[286] Park Chan-wook,[287] or any other creator of note— is difficult. Selling it is less so. Art need not always be attractive: Bosch's paintings were frequently grotesque[288] as were Grosz's visual ridicule of the Weimar Republic.[289] Nor must they always be complex: The music of Debussy[290] and the ink paintings of Xu Beihong[291] *seem* simple enough for almost anyone to create (until they try). But there is a certain degree of skill supporting any art worthy of the name, even if the apparency of that skill is obscured by the simplest of presentations of the most modest of subjects. Spotting this—the quality of the thing—requires both careful examination and an understanding of art that not all causal observers will possess at the highest level.

Conversely, creating bullshit is easy, but the art is in the deal. The art is in the process of substituting the mediocre for the excellent, the repulsive for the appealing, and the wrong and false for the true and beautiful. This is the art of making many copies of planet earth's most common object—the fool.

For those who *can* detect quality, trash is obvious. The only requisites for developing an eye to distinguish the junk from the gems are dedication to study, an interest in the media and content about which one is learning, and access to material that is freely available online.[292] This is *elite* in that only a few are willing to invest themselves enough to achieve competence, but in no other way.

For those who cannot or will not educate themselves, there is no choice but to rely upon the opinions of experts, the wisdom of crowds, or their guts. Experts can be bought or fooled,[293] and the wisdom of crowds varies according to the crowd chosen.[294] There are worse options than relying upon gut feeling—one's instinctive appreciation for beauty [295] and authenticity[296]—but one man's gut differs from another. And although the gut is not often entirely wrong, it is rarely inclined to favor restraint. Decisions made accordingly are fine for Lamborghini-driving sheiks or the junk-food-loving billionaires of Silicon Valley—people who derive their power from their wealth and the land or companies they own (the capitalists in the Marxist framework)[297]—but for the national elite, such garishness will not do.

One might imagine that the extensive and expensive educations of the national elite would inoculate them to the machinations of grifters. One would be wrong. Brand-name educations are not necessarily of substance—one can study nonsense extensively. And those whose worth within society is solely dependent upon them *being better in the general sense, but not in any domain in particular* are more easily manipulated by fads, tricksters, and smooth talkers than almost anyone else.

For one who must be *better* in a way no one can unambiguously define, tastes are so interwoven with merit that to trust one's instincts or personal opinions is to hazard a loss of prestige (the only currency and reserve of many of the national elite). Beauty can be seen, but not fully perceived, by those unable to acknowledge that there are things and people greater than themselves. The singularly narcissistic can only look inward—outside of their *awesome awesomeness* they can imagine nothing of worth—and appreciating beauty in the fullest sense, the sense of awe, is something forever prohibited by their egos.[298] This is the mental condition of the national elite, collectively—if not always individually. Thus, *fashion over beauty*, and fashion can be shockingly ugly.[299]

There are few better examples of this distorted sense of aesthetic value than *The Physical Impossibility of Death in the Mind of Someone Living*—a tiger shark carcass suspended in a tank filled with a formaldehyde solution—billed and sold as a sculpture by artist Damien Hirst.[300] Given that he made between 8 and 12 million USD for this piece, Hirst has demonstrated competence in business.[301] Yet his skills in taxidermy may not be equivalent—the installation's shark had to be replaced due to decomposition. (Hirst has asserted that this was partially the result of an error on the part of curators.)

Hirst is British, as are many of the buyers of his art.[302] Still, the lesson of marketing holds. Jeff Koons, probably best known for his balloon animal sculptures and *Michael Jackson and Bubbles* (a ceramic statue of Jackson and his pet chimpanzee that sold for 6.5 million USD in 2001), is most certainly an American.[303] If he is a sculptor is less certain—he often *conceptualizes* the works sold under his name but has others do the actual construction. (There is nothing more American than outsourcing![304])

Considering the obviousness of the works and the way contemporary artists present themselves, a pattern emerges: The pinnacle of artistic success—at least in the financial sense—is reached not by practicing the skills of one's nominal art, but by developing a different talent entirely—that of projecting supreme (and possibly a touch psychopathic) conviction in one's genius and vision while in the company of those of the highest station *and subtly mocking them and taking their money.*

This is an art unto itself. And it can be applied to almost any domain. The skillful bullshit artist essentially replicates the class-level actions of the national elite but with *flair* and *style*. There is a distinct possibility that a considerable minority within the national elite (or at least some gallery curators) recognize this—making the con a *meta/self-con* of sorts—and so admire the audacity of the premier artist that they are willing to subsidize his charlatanism with a wink and nod.[305]

There is also the distinct possibility that both artist and elite alike tacitly acknowledge that what is being bought and sold is, depending upon circumstances and expense, either a late-stage capitalist[306] act of conspicuous consumption (with the transaction itself being performative) or collaborative chicanery intended to deceive the public into believing that the elite can appreciate that which lesser mortal cannot.

Or the elite could be gullible idiots.

Either way, the recipe for taking elite money and transforming it into *your money* remains unchanged. This is making a cake without having to preheat your oven.[307]

Plan of Action/Recipe for Success

1. Find something ordinary, ugly, or *slightly* iconic (but in a lower class/pedestrian way).[308]

2. Ironically repurpose the thing or design, making it bigger, smaller, odder, or vaguely off-putting. If the item in question is an example of good industrial design, distort and deform it so that its elegance is lost.

3. Develop an eccentric, enigmatic, or ambiguously hostile persona. Choose clothing and personal effects that

resemble those that one would expect to see on a construction worker circa 1950, a Cuban revolutionary, or a homeless person. If you cannot manage this because of personal insecurity a) become more confident or b) buy a suit and wear it *everywhere*.[309]

4. Start showing your work at places singularly ill-suited to refinement and sophistication. Preferably, these places should be old and/or in a state of disuse. Vacant industrial facilities are one option. Derelict schools, prisons, or asylums are others.[310] To have a proper showing, you will need other *artists* to collaborate with you (more about that later), so start looking for them if you do not presently know of several.

5. Find someone who is *already* conning the elites, build a relationship with that person, and get that person's endorsement.

6. Cultivate a skillset in the fields of dissembling, rhetoric, and verbal redirection. Perfect the art of saying nothing at length and with irony and misplaced emotional intensity.

7. Practice considering and describing every part of your life, no matter how mundane or indistinct from that of any other person, as *performance art*. The only absolute distinction between art and life is that art has a frame.[311] Frame everything!

8. When you finally achieve some modicum of success, immediately assume an attitude of indifference or reservation. *I do not want to become too commercial!* you must protest while ratcheting the price of your product (meaning *you*) to stratospheric levels.

9. Be on time to nothing. Peasants scurry from one assignment to the next. But the meeting starts when the great man arrives. Or if going for the French intellectual effect (always a challenge for those without gallic blood, but worth considering), show up disheveled and moderately intoxicated.[312]

10. Periodically destroy what you have created, preferably in the most public manner possible.[313] Declare that either no one has understood the message you meant to send (with the subtext being that they are too stupid to deduce the meaning on their own, and you are too important to explain it) or that the work simply does not meet your ridiculously high standards.

With only slight modification, you can apply this process to anything—including cults and multi-level marketing schemes (which can sometimes be one and the same).[314] The thing that matters most: Your confidence. Never lose sight of that, and you will be able to make fools of more elite than you likely imagine possible.

The purpose of the artistic and cultish approach is threefold: First, it allows you to take money from those who have too much and give it to someone who has too little—*you!* Second, it allows you to further unmoor the elite from reality. And the more gullible they become, the more easily executed the *Substitution Theory Tactic 3 (ST Tactic: 3)* becomes. Third, it undermines the credibility of the elites. The more moronic their investments, the more warped their aristocratic appetites become, the bigger fools they appear to be.

Keep this in mind when applying this tactic: If enough people *say* something is art, it likely is. Feel no guilt about lining your wallet.

ST Tactic 3 (Disinformation): Insinuation, Implantation, Irresistibility, and Inconsistency

Identifying Ignorance and Bottlenecks of Information Flow

Faking elite status is difficult. It can be done.[315] But this is a *grift*, not a means of effecting change. The right approach is different. If you want to mislead the elite effectively, *flatter them just enough and in just the right way*. This requires a certain delicacy and understanding of human nature, but nothing beyond the abilities of the reasonably intelligent man.

To be a member of the national elite is to take a certain pride in a particular kind of ignorance—a willful ignorance that separates higher beings from the hoi polloi. A less substantial version of this ignorance can be seen in those who refuse to learn how to use a smartphone, who profess no knowledge of popular culture, and who would have you believe that they have never been inside a Walmart.[316] This is *prestige ignorance*, and although it may be exaggerated by those who possess it, such does not make it false. This ignorance is weakness, as ignorance always is.

The national elite understand little about the mindset of the average American. And if they are to maintain their position in life, they cannot risk learning too much in too obvious a manner. From birth to school to work to selecting a family and community, the elite are kept away from their inferiors and have no real opportunity to get to know much about them. This was not always the case, but as America has urbanized and suburbanized and social mobility within the country has declined, the perspective and shared-culture gap between the haves and have-nots has widened. *Coming Apart*, a book written nearly ten years ago, describes the mechanics of this quite well.[317] And however extreme the rift was then, it has likely grown. Inequality in the United States demonstrably has.[318]

So how do the national elite understand their subjects? They rely on social and data science for one—surveys, analyses of web traffic and websites—and they rely on *casual informers.* These are the few peasants in the national elite's circles, or even anywhere in proximity to them. These are the plumbers, the electricians, the doormen, and the security staff who serve and protect the national elite (if only from annoying teenagers and leaky faucets).

The process of gathering information from such casual informers is complicated by the discomfort the national elite may have in communicating with those outside their class—or rather, their *subset of the middle class,* with *middle class* being what all but a few Americans consider themselves to be.[319] And they likely overestimate differences in language, vocabulary, and communication style between the elite and non-elite (which, combined with their desire to establish their secular moral superiority, can make them seem quite patronizing).[320]

The role of the casual informer is diminished by none of this; however, it does increase the odds that the casual informer does *not know that he is serving as a casual informer.* It is the nature of the ideologically trained to be both bombastic on the podium and dithering in the flesh. A true ideologue (or anyone trying to make a living by passing as one) cannot speak of too much with surety. He can recite the accepted views, he can compare the major schools of thought within his belief, but he must be circumspect. If he thinks or speaks too much without the appropriate guidance or textual support, he may violate some tenant or technical requirement, however obscure, of the godless religion that butters his brioche.[321]

So the casual informer/plumber/worker is likely to find himself being asked questions in the most roundabout of ways, questions about what he thinks of these *newfangled electric cars*. (The plumber has one, but he lets his daughter drive it: Plumbing pays adequately.[322]) Or his opinion on environmental concerns or immigration may be solicited, but indirectly, always indirectly.

These informal interviews are an excellent opportunity for the responsible citizen to implant irresistible disinformation into the mind of the targeted elite, and if delivered with a cultivated *aw-shucks* apparent authenticity, the untruths will prove sticky.

Now, we must consider two relevant aspects of this plan: First is the nature of the deception. Second are the viable mechanisms of infiltration.

Deception: Lies, Exaggerations, and the Trust Ladder

The best lies are largely true. And the best liars establish trust and then increase the degree of their deception over time. This is the strategy used by every competent confidence man. The *casual informer/infiltrator* should apply fundamentally similar techniques.

The idea is this: Be *trustworthy* on anything that can be positively disproven. This includes factual statements and broad assertions about the politics or the state of the world. Most importantly, it pertains to the professional conduct of the casual informer—timeliness, courtesy, quality of work, fairness of billing procedures, and warrantying. Providing good workmanship at a reasonable rate and with a respectful disposition is the fastest way for the infiltrator to build trust.

And this proper conduct must be maintained for the duration of the ruse.

As the good reputation of the infiltrator grows, he will likely be given more referrals—and these will allow more access to the homes and ears of the national elite. *Homophily*—preference for those like oneself—is a fundamental aspect of human nature.[323] And people of a certain class, particularly the elite, are more likely to trust those recommended to them by their peers than those who have no connection to the in-group.

This process—that of building relationships with the target group and expanding the network of relationships within that group—is that of climbing the trust ladder. And the higher one climbs, the more misinformation he can spread. As is often the case with ladders, the most difficult process is that of getting one's foot on the first rung. To do this, one must be in the *right place at the right time*, meaning in proximity to certain neighborhoods and willing and able (licensed, bonded, insured, etc.) to provide critical services. While there is no definitive list of national elite hotspots, the cities and communities below would appear to be ideal targets for infiltration:

1. Washington, D.C.—The political significance of this city is obvious, but one should keep in mind that much of the city is not rich and many communities have little connection to the world of the national elite. Georgetown and Chevy Chase both appear to be prosperous and with a considerable number of elites, but if these are the ideal communities for the infiltrator to focus his attention is difficult to ascertain purely from online research.[324]

2. New York City—Again, most of the city has no connection to politics, and the cost of living in the City is high.[325] One should distinguish between the many millionaires of the

City (the majority of whom have little political pull) and actual shapers of policy and opinion.

3. New Haven, Connecticut—The home of Yale University, its connection to the world of policy and power should be obvious.

4. Cambridge, Massachusetts—Harvard University and the Massachusetts Institute of Technology. The significance of the people in these communities in shaping world events would be difficult to overestimate.

5. Stanford, California—The Left Coast and the Midwest (meaning Chicago for these purposes) are not as closely connected to the power structure as are the East Coast cities, but that is not to say that they are without consequence. Stanford is a good candidate for infiltration due to its university, which is the closest that California has to an Ivy League school.

This list of locations is not definitive, nor should the dedicated casual informer/infiltrator/activist assume that one *must* work or live in a major metropolitan area to efficiently achieve his ends. The power structure of the United States is urbanized, but not to the degree found in many countries.

In Japan, one of the best universities (University of Tokyo),[326] the center of government,[327] and major producers of cultural content (Toho[328]—Japan's largest film studio—many publishers,[329] and many anime studios[330]), are all within one city. In China, Beijing is both the capital city and the home of the best universities (Tsinghua and Peking)[331]. And it is upon the Beijing dialect that Standard Chinese is based.[332] In France, the same pattern applies—the nation's best universities (Paris Sciences et Lettres University, Ecole Polytechnique, and

Sorbonne University),[333] the nation's center of government,[334] and the prestige dialect (Parisian French)[335] are all in the City of Lights.

But the United States is different. Washington is not the home of America's best schools, nor is Standard American English (to the extent it exists) based on the dialect of that city.[336] In the realm of media, the country has not one center, but three—New York, Los Angeles, and Nashville,[337] with other cities, such as Atlanta, of increasing importance.[338] This makes infiltrating the national elite a bit easier. They may have all attended the same colleges, but outside of that bottleneck, they are scattered across communities throughout the United States.

This means that the determined infiltrator may not need to travel far. He can direct his attention to select communities that are no more than a few hours' drive away. And this would likely be preferable to long-distance relocation as it requires little in the development of a cover story: A plumber from Clarksville, Tennessee, is less likely to arouse suspicion when working in Nashville than he would when working in Chicago. He is also saved the time of moving his licenses and professional credentials from one state to the next.

Compiling a list of every community of influence in the United States would be impractical for this text, but finding a local center of power—where at least some of the national elite live—should not be too difficult for anyone so determined. The national elite are usually *not* the richest members of a given community, and they are unlikely to casually flex their status— such is an undignified act, unsuited to those with real power.[339]

Respected universities will attract a few national elites, even if they (school and/or elites) are not of the highest caliber: Academia is a strange country. Its centers of prestige are few,

122

but influential academics are spread over a larger area. (Just because one *went* to a prestigious school, does not mean one can get tenure there.[340]) And certain private organizations not part of the government/East Coast academic structure—the RAND Corporation, for example—can wield quite a bit of influence.[341]

The infiltrator must always keep his eyes and ears open. Opportunities to shift the course of history, however slightly, may be closer than they first appear.

Breadcrumbs, Hags, and the Saltine Cracker House

Who, *how*, and *where* to deceive have been addressed. But regarding *what*? The envelope has postage and a label on it, but there is nothing inside.

Rather than advocating a specific set of lies (which would lead to repetition of content and eventual detection of casual informers/infiltrators), this section includes a few major concepts to be broadly applied so that the infiltrator can develop his own narratives and instruments for promoting confusion.

Breadcrumbs[342]—Few will willingly leave the comfort of their established beliefs without some guarantee of safe means of return. Thus, *breadcrumbs* are critical. These are statements, assertions, or generally agreed-upon facts or ideological tenants that provide the target with a visible connection to existing beliefs—markers for the path home. The infiltrator should listen first and foremost and only after identifying the critical core of the target's beliefs, acknowledge and confirm these beliefs while gradually leading the target down the path of confusion.

Hags—Nothing brings people together like a common enemy. The *hag* should be whatever it is that the target despises. The *hag du jour* has been Trump—evil incarnate, who locks immigrant children in cages[343] before fattening them with government peanut butter[344] and pushing them into the tortilla oven (he likes Mexican *if not Mexicans*, it seems). This hag has largely retired. New hags may be *extremists* (however vaguely defined), Vladimir Putin, or any other prominent person or group who may act contrary to the will of the national elite.[345] At least some of the hags of the future are likely to be associated with the Chinese people or government, but *who* specifically is uncertain.[346] The only certain thing is that there *will* be a hag. The national elite need a hag to maintain a shared narrative and a shared goal—to defeat the ugliness (and replace it with an ugliness of their own).

The Saltine Cracker House—Without temptation, there can be no deception. But the temptation must not be *too delectable*. The odds that a casual informer/infiltrator would stumble upon a great conspiracy are slim. The target must not be offered something impossibly good. It is easy to resist ridiculous fantasies. Rather, the infiltrator should offer not the entire meal of a grand narrative, but a few crackers instead—suggestions that someone, somewhere is planning something, acting against the interests of the elite, or otherwise likely to pose a problem. Switching metaphors: The monster is scarier when it is never fully seen.[347] Godzilla's footprints and his distant roar rattle the nerves more deeply than seeing him in a boxing match with his shiny mecha-doppelgänger.[348] *This* is the power of imagination. A good infiltrator does no more work than needed. He hints, he nudges, and he lets the target's mind grow terrified of sounds and shadows.

Nothing *too* good must be presented. Offer the target saltines. Offer him something *satisfactory*. Let his hunger, not your excellence in the culinary arts, provide the seasoning. Do this and watch him grow more ravenous and more careless by the day.

The Trap Avoided

The reason for creating this text was simple: to help America (and the world) rout a march towards Armageddon.[349] *Armageddon* being a hot war between China and the United States—two nuclear powers. The theory contained herein is only somewhat more complex. And the suggested tactics are meant merely to serve as starting points, to be expanded and refined by the creative and the determined in ways beyond the imaginings and comprehension of the author.

This text advocates the destruction of nothing and no one (aside from a few illusions *and delusions* of competence). Rather, the tools herein are meant to be used to buy time, enough time for the balance of global power to shift. They are not against the natural flow of things: They rely almost exclusively on accelerating and redirecting existing cultural trends. The world order of the future is likely multipolar, with five major nations (the United States, China, Russia, Japan, and India) having large but rarely overlapping spheres of influence.[350] This does not pose an existential threat to America, and there is no reason to believe that China, Russia, Japan, and India each having domains independent of United States control will cause any harm to the American people.

The destination is fine, but the road there is likely to be rocky.

The American national elite have reigned over a major portion of the globe since the 1950s and were without peer from the collapse of the Soviet Union to 2019.[351] From this much power comes arrogance and entitlement. The national elite will not take kindly to being reduced to one amongst many. And this is where we—responsible American citizens—come into service. We can confuse, we can obfuscate, we can annoy, and we can delay. This is our potential for a lasting contribution to the world. This should be our legacy.

The Trap does not block every path. We can guide our nation around it. Perhaps some other people will spring the Trap another time, but the evils of the day are more than sufficient.[352]

We—*you*—stand between peace and war, between tolerable and intolerable futures. And we do not need to be excellent in our endeavor, just good enough to buy time.

The Questions

Do you care enough to stand, to toil for peace? Or will you do nothing? Will you let the elite sacrifice our nation and the world on the altar of their fears, their greed, and their egomania?

These are not rhetorical. Consider them with care.

How you answer them matters.

The Last Chance Corps
(Redeeming the Unsavory Element)

There is nothing inherently wrong with punishment, even of the most brutal sort, but we must offer those who have erred the chance to redeem themselves if we expect them to be anything other than habitual criminals and lifelong burdens on society. Sacrifice is the road that leads from person disgraced to citizen restored.

The Problem

In the United States, 8 percent of the population has at least one felony conviction,[1] and far more have criminal records of some form.[2] Some of these people have not served prison time—pre-trial diversion and probation are relatively common for certain crimes—but that is not to say they escaped punishment or that they are not being punished still.

More than 60 percent of employers check arrest and conviction records for *all* potential employees, with most indicating that an arrest record reduces the likelihood of hiring a candidate *even if the charges were dismissed or the candidate was acquitted at trial*.[3] And a criminal conviction of any kind diminishes the chances of receiving a job offer by half.[4]

A felony conviction is almost certain to have a more significant effect, with felons being barred from a great many professions. We may have reason enough to prevent a convicted murderer from running a daycare center. But restrictions do not end there.[5] Depending upon the state, a felon may be forbidden from becoming an acupuncturist,[6] an athletic trainer,[7] a boxer,[8] a massage therapist, a clinical psychologist, a radiographer, a social worker, a veterinarian,[9] or any one of many other professions. And without expungement (a complex, expensive, and inconsistently available process) or pardon, this disability rarely goes away. There is no cure. Convicted felons face other constraints on voting rights,[10] housing access,[11] and international travel.[12]

This is the punishment after the punishment. And to a certain extent, we can do little about it. Arrest records, including those officially expunged or sealed, may show up on certain private databases years after the fact.[13] And asking the public to *forgive* and overlook convictions—to hire, to rent to, or to keep the company of identified criminals without bias or discrimination—is as absurd as it is unnatural. The American people are not particularly forgiving.[14] And there is no good reason for them to be so.

There are few more miserly in their compassion than those who wear their humanity on their sleeves. *Loves mankind, hates the individual*—most of us know the type. And even the most allegedly compassionate amongst us appear unable to look past an ill-worded tweet from one's teen years. Felons face poorer odds still.

Forgiveness is the wrong route—it relies upon grace, which is neither consistent in its application nor very likely to be sustainable for any length of time. The age of bleeding hearts and short prison sentences has come and gone,[15] and that era—running through a portion of the 1970s[16]—was not one to which very many would want to return.[17]

And forgiveness is worse still in that it does not restore *respect*—the currency of social interactions, be they of a personal or economic nature. Those who can and do forgive may well find that they cannot respect those they have forgiven. And this—a lack of respect—is a punishment of another form, one that can be deeply injurious to the personality and psyche of the disrespected.

There is also the tendency of some to confuse a soft heart with a soft head or a weak will—to assume that those predisposed to forgiveness are suckers, simps, or simply stupid. For these people, every act of forgiveness that benefits them is proof positive that they are just a bit smarter (and more adept at manipulation) than the granter of forgiveness.

Finally, there is the corrosiveness of groveling. The courts are filled with *sorry souls*—they are sorry for their crimes, their sins, their drinking, their mismanagement of money, and their neglect of their children. The better part of them are sorry for themselves most of all. And they are forever seeking forgiveness. Jesus, Mohammed, Yahweh, judges, and victims—*please, please, please forgive me! Show me compassion!*

Blah, blah blah . . .

This—the sad melodrama of repentance and mercy— hurts begged and beggar alike. With each scene of this fools' play, the beggar grows more manipulative and insincere and the begged grows more contemptuous. And by the time all is over, everyone involved is stained in heart and spirit.

So what is to be done? If the path of forgiveness only leads to cynicism, what can take us where we want and need to go— to the way of restored and productive citizens?

The Solution: The Last Chance Corps

Rather than forgiveness, mercy, or punishment without end, let us consider a fourth option: That those who have violated the social contract be given means to *earn* restoration of their rights and a fair measure of respect.

129

This is *not* punishment. And although it might stand to allow some long uncaught crimes to go unpunished (at least if implemented as suggested herein), it is not intended to serve in lieu of prison.

This process of redemption *cannot* be easy. By needs, it must be hard, exceedingly hard. Rights can be reacquired by legislation, by pardon, or by official forgetting (the destruction of formal documentation), but *respect* is another matter. Such is where *sacrifice* comes into play. With sufficient misery, risk, and contributions to the welfare of society, those who are less than zero may never be made *heroes*, but they can be cleansed of their sins in a purgatory of careful and useful design.

I propose that we, the American people, by way of our government, establish a group—the *Last Chance Corps*—that affords almost any American the hope of a clean slate. Debt; minor or serious criminal convictions; civil and criminal judgments, penalties, and fees owed; back taxes (anything except for sex crimes involving children)—all is erased after sufficient time and honorable service in the LCC.

The Process: LCC Induction, Experience, and Benefits

1. Any American citizen wishing to be free from his or her past applies to the LCC and provides complete documentation of debt owed; criminal convictions; unpaid fines, support obligations, and judgments; back taxes; and the nature of any punishment received (duration, correctional facility where served, etc.).

2. The appropriate official in the LCC verifies all records and checks for outstanding warrants and ongoing criminal investigations. If the applicant is found to be neither a

130

suspect, wanted, nor a perpetrator of sex crimes against children, he (or she) can advance to induction.

3. The nature of the LCC, the work it does, the rights surrendered by those who join the LCC, and the specific benefits one receives for serving in the LCC and how and when those benefits are awarded—these are explained to the inductee.

4. The inductee undergoes training, becomes an *LC Corpsman*, and is assigned whatever tasks are deemed to be suitable to the abilities of the person and to be necessary for the improvement of the nation.

5. The term of service, of at least five years but no more than 15 years, begins.

Terms, Benefits, and Limitations of Service

The Terms of Service

1. Any person who joins the LCC waives completely and perpetually the right to make any civil or criminal claim against the LCC.

2. Any person who joins the LCC surrenders all property, rights to inheritance, and rights of name and identity to the LCC.

3. The LCC retains the absolute right to assign any LC Corpsman any task of any form that is deemed to be to the public benefit, regardless of risks to the LC Corpsman's safety, survival, or sanity.

4. Refusal to obey any valid order by the designated officers or commanders of the LCC shall result in punishments to be determined by the LCC, with no recourse to the ordinary courts or military tribunals. Refusal may also

result in dismissal from the LCC and loss of any benefits derived from service. No surrendered property shall be returned to the dismissed LC Corpsman.

5. The benefits of joining the LCC do not reach maturity until the term of service is honorably completed.

6. The duration of the inductee's term of service is determined by the LCC and based upon the severity of the crimes committed by the inductee, the amount of money owed by the inductee, and the nature of the debts/judgments against the inductee.

The Benefits of Service

1. Food, clothing, housing, and rudimentary healthcare are provided by the LCC.

2. A one-time payment of between 25,000 and 75,000 dollars (to be periodically adjusted for inflation), depending upon the length of service, is awarded to those who fulfill their service obligation to the LCC.

3. A new identity is provided upon honorable completion of service.

The Limitations of Service

1. No member of the LCC will have any discretion in the labor assigned to him (or her).

2. No member of the LCC will have any rights to freedom of movement, religion, or speech/communications for the duration of the service agreement.

3. No member of the LCC will have any protection under labor or safety regulations that apply to civilians/members of the military.

4. No member of the LCC will receive excuse or pardon from future criminal conduct, debts, or tortuous actions.

The Takeaway

The Last Chance Corps would offer a new identity and 5,000 dollars per year to those who serve in it.

In exchange for this, the LCC inductee would be required to surrender, at the time of acceptance to the LCC, *everything* from his or her old life. Upon successful completion of the member's service, the LC Corpsman is simply declared *dead* by the federal government. No debts, obligations, judgments, criminal investigations, or convictions may follow the LC Corpsman from one life to the next. Nor do any academic or professional records, rights to inheritance, or intellectual property.

This is a clean slate in the strictest sense. Those who wish to start anew (and are willing to sacrifice for the opportunity to do so) have their second chance at life, but picking and choosing what shall be kept and what shall be discarded is something the LC Corpsman cannot do.

An Ideal: Tough but Fair

Way I see it, that's because you're tough, but you're fair. You're all about justice.

"Mijo," *Better Call Saul* (Gould & MacLaren, 2015)

This proposal is not overly lenient. Such is a matter of necessity. We must establish to all—victims, creditors, courts, prosecutors, the public, and (most of all) perpetrators themselves—that the LCC offers neither forgiveness nor mercy. Instead, it offers a chance for one to *earn* a fresh start. And the person who does so is no more beholden to society than would be any other free man or woman.

Next, two critical questions: *1) What sort of work could an LC Corpsman be assigned? 2) What should the LC Corpsman be expected to do to prove himself/herself?*

Extraordinarily high-risk military and security work come to mind—things so dicey no civilized nation would ever ask an ordinary soldier to do—but one should not focus on this option to the exclusion of others. We only need so many soldiers, expendable or otherwise. And war for the sake of amusement and folly only destabilizes a nation.

Consider these eight alternatives to martial service. They are but a few of the many possible opportunities for deliverance by blood and suffering:

1. Forest, mine, and industrial firefighting

2. Construction and maintenance work in ultra-hazardous environments (decaying weirs, levees, ordinary dams, or anywhere water and electricity are likely to meet)

3. Fast-track pharmaceutical and medical procedure testing

4. Cleaning and restoration of the most severely polluted environments, including ones contaminated with radiation or carcinogenic and teratogenic compounds

5. Disassembly of weapons of mass destruction

6. The unarmed tracking and capture of bloodthirsty fugitives

7. Engaging in last-chance search and rescue operations

8. Nearly suicidal undercover investigative work

Many would be injured when performing these tasks, and some would die. That is to be expected. This incumbent risk is what would make service in the LCC worthy of respect. The hazards, harms, and losses of life that occur in the LCC must be well-publicized so that the public, members of the legal community, and any inclined to join the LCC understand that it does not grant favors. It only affords an opportunity to the most determined.

Obstacles and Objections to Implementation

First, we must acknowledge that some who honorably serve in the LCC will return to their lives of debt, crime, and debauchery. This cannot be prevented. And we, as a people, must be willing to accept some possibility of relapse. There are no completely foolproof means of rehabilitation. If we insist on total certainty, we will deny the worthiest and least worthy alike the chance to redeem themselves.

Second, there is the chance that some crimes will go unpunished. As this proposal stands, the honorably discharged LC Corpsman is rewarded for his or her service with the death of the prior legal person. Any crimes and liabilities committed or incurred by the dead are without much in the way of remedy. Stated simply: One cannot prosecute the deceased. One can sue the *estate* of the deceased. And an estate would exist—with the LCC being the executor and sole beneficiary—but beyond that, the aggrieved would have little remedy.

This is a legitimate concern. Yet the benefits of the LCC to the majority of those who survive their service and to the public at large will outweigh this risk. A great many of those in need of liberation from their records and reputations—the ideal recruits—have more than one illegal action in their pasts. *Most* Americans, including those who have never been questioned by police, have committed a crime (and quite possibly more than one felony).[18] Without providing closure of their histories, few candidates would have much incentive to join the LCC.

And the public would lose great advantages as well. American infrastructure is collapsing, endangering lives and livelihoods ever more by the day.[19] There is extraordinarily unsafe work to be done to keep a society powered by high-energy fuel sources, heavy equipment, and noxious chemicals running. Our current techniques for containing and removing pollutants are not without their perils either. And in future times of pandemic—pandemics with the potential to be far more dangerous than that of 2020—expediency may dictate that vaccines and treatments that have undergone only the most limited animal testing be evaluated through human trials. These are the areas in which the LCC stands to offer society the most.

The greatest single obstacle to the establishment of the LCC is the United States Constitution. The extent to which a person may surrender his rights has yet to be fully tested. Even if a parallel system of justice unique to the LCC is implemented, it might be expected to observe some legal and constitutional norms, much as the military is expected to honor (to a limited extent) some constitutional rights under the Uniform Code of Military Justice.[20]

Seeking easily reversed Supreme Court decisions is not the optimal method to ensure that the LCC be allowed to operate with the latitude it requires to be effective. One could make an argument for *consent*—that those who join the LCC *consent* to the loss of their rights and thus have no redress—but this is a legally uncertain line of argument. Particularly if the courts find agreements between the inductee (including agreements to submit to the LCC tribunals) to be *unconscionable*, the LCC will be neutered.

A better approach is a constitutional amendment giving the LCC extraordinary leeway to operate as it sees fit. This would proactively nullify any constitutional attacks and would allow the LCC and its policies to stand on a sure footing. Additionally, an LCC amendment could establish the right of the LCC to declare a person *legally dead* and could compel creditors, investigators, and the state and federal courts to honor this declaration.

Constitutional amendments are not easily had, nor should they be, but the LCC and its benefits to those in need of redemption and society itself would make improving America's foundational legal document worth the effort.

Finally, there is the problem of uncovered identities—the discovery of the last-life legal personality of an honorably discharged LC Corpsman. This is not only possible, but increasingly likely with advancements in facial recognition, mass surveillance, and genetic testing. Yet that does not negate the benefits or purpose of the LCC. It does not change the legal standing of the new person. And the almost unbearably grueling and consistently miserable experience of surviving (or attempting to survive) a term of service in the LCC should allow the LC Corpsman to gain the respect of most, even if his former self is revealed.

Sensible Limits and Moderate Protections

While a great many LC Corpsmen will be maimed or killed in the line of duty, the majority need to survive for the program to attract a significant number of participants. Rather than burdening the LCC with specific safety regulations, the government should simply place certain reasonable limits on total permanent injuries and deaths suffered by LC Corpsmen. The exact upper limit is open to debate, but one can look to

Romans and their idea of *decimation* (literally, *removal of a tenth*) for a very general idea of how much death is *too* much death.

Ideally, no more than 10 percent of LC Corpsmen should die in the line of duty, and not many more should be permanently disabled. As for the potential cost of the last— paying for those who have been harmed during their service— the simplest and most economical route is to declare that injuries incurred while a member of the LCC *do not* make one eligible for state or federal disability benefits. This condition could be included in the LCC amendment.

A sensible and humane alternative to conventional disability compensation would be to provide LC Corpsmen seriously, permanently, and *unwillingly* injured payment for the portion of their time served and the same legal death and rebirth offered to those who have completed the entirety of their contracts. The conditional of the previous sentence— *unwillingly*—is critical, as some LC Corpsmen might find the incentive to injure themselves in exchange for a shorter contract (and the attendant benefits) too great to ignore.

The Path Forward

Without focused effort and dedication, the LCC and the opportunity for renewal and respect it would provide disgraced, debt-ridden, and criminal Americans will forever remain a fantasy. But inertia is not inevitable. All that this proposal offers is the skeleton of a marvelous and novel beast. The internal organs, flesh, and hair remain undeveloped.

Probably the closest the LCC has to an ancestor is the French Foreign Legion, which allows inductees to take assumed names and offers those wounded in action the immediate opportunity to become French by virtue of spilt blood (*Français par le sang verse.*). LC Corpsmen are offered a similar chance at atonement, but one should not overstate how much the LCC and the *Légion étrangère* have in common.

And the traditions, customs, and proven practices of the L.É. are likely to serve as imperfect patterns for the organization and disciplinary systems of the LCC.

Thus, we end at the *beginning*—the beginning of a serious consideration as to how and to what extent absolution can and should be earned in our society, how much one can (and should) sacrifice for respect, and how those in need of a chance to prove their worth and society at large can come to a sustainable and mutually beneficial agreement.

And there is another beginning still—one in which others take the initiative to further develop the ideas herein, to share them, and to encourage their peers to consider and contribute to them as well—that beginning is the responsibility of the reader. That beginning will never come to pass without the work of millions, without whom we shall not evolve beyond the tomfoolery of forgiveness and mercy and towards a model of justice founded on sacrifice, decency, and opportunity.

That beginning—that first step towards the greatness and wonder that the LCC stands to be—will never happen without you.

Student Loans and a Means of Reform

Showing compassion to those who have made bad decisions does not require that we allow them to profit at the expense of blameless taxpayers.

Over the last year, calls for mass forgiveness of student loans have grown louder. While this debt is a pulverizing burden for millions of Americans, outright loan forgiveness is profoundly unfair to both the taxpayer and to all who have dutifully honored their financial obligations.

I agree with the argument that the current loan system is flawed and in need of reform, and I understand that some people are simply unable to repay their loans and will remain forever so close to destitution that attempts to extract anything more than a pittance from them will prove futile.

So what is to be done?

I propose that the bankruptcy code be amended so that government-backed student loans can be discharged under Chapter 7 with relative ease. This can be done in such a way that people who need debt relief are neither enriched nor abused by the legal process. The requirements for discharging this debt should be the same as those for discharging other consumer debts, with a few minor modifications. Here are the specific conditions I advocate be added to 11 U.S.C. § 7 to make the student loan discharge system fair and equitable:

(a) Any person who has more than 50% of his/her government-backed student debt discharged shall:

    (1) be forever barred from receiving additional government-backed student loans;

(2) surrender all credentials, proof of academic completion, professional licenses dependent upon formal education (medical licenses, legal licenses, teaching licenses, nursing licenses, etc.), and academic titles and honors;

(3) agree to refrain from using any academic pre- or post-nominal (Ph.D., J.D., M.D., etc.) for professional purposes, with the understanding that he/she may be held in contempt of court for using such titles for economic gain;

(4) surrender completely and without restriction all intellectual property created in the course of completing his/her degree (including dissertations, theses, research documents, patents, electronic media, etc.) to the United States Department of Education, which shall assume ownership of said intellectual property.

(b) Upon notification of any student or former student having had more than 50% of his/her government-backed student debt discharged, any higher educational institution eligible to receive Title IV funds shall:

(1) delete or otherwise destroy the academic and behavioral transcripts of said student;

(2) remove said student from all alumni/graduate lists;

(3) immediately transfer copies of any intellectual property that was created by the student in the course of completing his/her degree (and is in the possession of the institution) to the United States Department of Education.

(c) If intellectual property created by the person who is seeking to have more than 50% of his/her government-backed student debt discharged is found by the court to be a joint creation of that person and another person or entity, the court shall determine what portion, section, or percentage of that property was created by the bankrupt person and shall order that share of the property interest transferred to the United States Department of Education, with the rights of the remaining intellectual property holders being unaffected.

These simple additions to 11 U.S.C. § 7 would allow for the legitimately overburdened to be free of debt while discouraging anyone who would seek to engorge himself (or herself) at the expense of the nation.

Finally, I advocate that student loan debt restructuring be facilitated under 11 U.S.C. § 13, with the following simple additions to the law:

(a) that any person who seeks relief under 11 U.S.C. § 13 for student loan debt agrees to pay at least 50 percent of his/her disposable income to the relevant creditors either until the loan is completely repaid or for a period of 10 years (whichever is shorter);

(b) that any person who seeks relief under 11 U.S.C. § 13 for student loan debt agrees to perform at least 15 hours of unpaid national service per week, of a type to be determined by the court, for a period of 10 years or until the loan is fully repaid (whichever is shorter).

I invite readers to consider this proposal. If they find it to be reasonable, they should feel free to copy all (or part) of this document into a letter directed to the appropriate officials.

The Law Must Die

The American system of statutes, regulations, executive orders, guidance documents and directives, and case law has grown too unwieldy to be applied or interpreted fairly and consistently. The problem is complex. The solution is comparatively simple.

Introduction

Every law, every regulation, every executive order, and every binding court decision is enforced by violence or the threat thereof. *Any* law or regulation, be it a statute prohibiting murder, rape, arson, robbery, growing grass above an approved length,[1] or selling individual cigarettes without a license,[2] grants the agents of the state however much force they deem necessary (up to killing the non-compliant) to prohibit or compel an action. More than that, each new mandate invites the state further into the lives of its citizens for ever more detailed investigation. Thus, the pretextual traffic stop[3] can easily turn into detention, search, and arrest, and the missing house number can be used as an excuse to harass someone to the point of leaving a community.[4]

The American *governments* (federal, state, and local) have vast powers and enormous armories,[5] with even the smallest law enforcement agencies having enough materiel to establish paramilitary units.[6] And as the law extends its reach, the mechanisms of enforcement likewise extend their grasp.

Beyond the constant threat of state violence, there is the issue of perpetual punishment. The accumulation of laws allows for almost anyone[7] to become entrapped in a system of arrest, trial, *correction*, and subsequent unemployability that is no less adept at creating return clients[8] than it is at preventing recidivism.

The Problem: Inconsistency and Impossibility

At present, the number of federal laws is unknown, with an estimate from the early 1980s putting the number somewhat above 3,000.[9] And this does not include legally binding regulations created at the rulemaking level,[10] which requires a public review process but no congressional hearings or votes. Nor does it include "interpretative rules, general statements of policy, or rules of agency, organization, procedure, or practice," which are implemented entirely without public oversight.[11]

Estimating the number of state laws is even more difficult. The most recent (2020) print edition of West's Annotated California Codes runs to approximately 450 books and costs slightly more than 20,000 USD.[12] Granted, California is an outlier, with most states having shorter annotated codes, but such does not establish that understanding the laws of those states is any easier, and certainly not if those states lean more heavily on the tradition of case law than on legislative codification—with the latter being what California seems to favor. Not every law is enforced (or enforced consistently), but the authority these laws grant the enforcers roaming our streets and collecting government salaries to interfere in the daily activities of the citizenry remains ever ready.[13]

One cause of this overabundance of statutes is the nature of legislatures and their function. *Legislative productivity*— the number of substantial (non-ceremonial) laws passed by a governing body—is treated as a measure of the body's effectiveness, with the idea being *the more laws passed, the better,*[14] and legislatures (and legislators) that *do not* pass a great many laws should be viewed as ineffective.[15] Admittedly, there is a straightforward logic to this. If a legislature *is not* passing laws, what exactly is it doing? And why should its members be compensated?

Were an uncountable number of statutes not burdensome enough, there is the equally hefty matter of state and federal appellate court judges vying for promotion by virtue of their ability to craft decisions so incomprehensible that no one dare question them.[16] And these become part of the legal canon— meaning that *we* (or those of us in the relevant circuit) are bound by them. The predicament of judicial writings so verbose as to discomfit even the most determined and sharp-eyed of legal eagles is not limited to the United States, but it is almost exclusively one of countries that rely upon the common law system—with Australia, the United States, Canada, India, and the United Kingdom taking five of the seven top spots for world's longest written court opinions.[17]

As it stands now, our legal system is ungainly to the extent that not many police, few lawyers, and even fewer judges are entirely confident of what the laws they are supposed to enforce and interpret mean. Yet *ignorantia juris non excusat*—we are duty bound to know such a great many laws that no man or woman could live long enough to read them all.[18] This is especially problematic for actions that are merely *malum prohibitum*—prohibited legally, but not morally wrong in the most obvious sense—rather than *malum in se*.

Our laws are enforced inconsistently because *they must be.* As bad as this is, a flawless and fair application of every statute, regulation, and court decision would be far worse. Were an impartial and perfectly reliable system of investigation, arrest, and prosecution to be designed and deployed, the populace would face near-constant interaction with the legal system.

The courts would collapse under dockets so weighty that the only means of repair would be to drag every barely-passed-the-bar *University of American Samoa* law school graduate[19] to a courtroom and assign him/her/zher a judgeship (or to coerce *even more* defendants into accepting plea bargains).[20] And the better portion of our schools would need to be converted from prison-preparation centers into proper penal facilities.[21]

A capricious gang acting under color of law that (more or less) maintains order or an unprejudiced engine of (in)justice that throws off its flywheel and grinds to a halt brief moments after redlining—this is not so much Hobson's choice as it is Sophie's.

Here is the root of the problem, simply restated: There are many reasons to expand the body of rationalizations for the leviathan's violence and almost none to contract said body. Here is the best fix: Laws, opinions, and regulations that do not live forever.

The Solution: Implementation and Effects

Attorneys gain clients and billable hours as the legal process grows more confusing. Legislators, many of whom are also attorneys, have reason to *pass laws*—the need to be *productive* and to increase their popularity by way of *getting tough on crime*—but almost none to *repeal* them.[22] Rulemaking divisions of the executive branch face pressures of their own. Even the members of the legislature inclined to prune the legal code will face either indifference from their peers or hostility from government agencies, police,[23] or some klatch of blue-haired church ladies terrified that *selling a motor vehicle on Sunday*[24] will lead one down the devil's path (much like metal music).[25]

Rather than expecting our legislators to *fix the system* by consistently acting against their rational self-interest, the simplest method of inhibiting the tumorous and deforming growth of government control is to give all laws, statutes, judicial opinions, regulatory decisions, and unofficial policy interpretation documents an expiration date. Twenty years might well be a sensible lifespan, but the exact number of years a law or interpretation thereof survives is less important than the mechanism of automatic termination. The model described in this proposal is somewhat like *sunsetting,* but with a greater number of mechanisms in place to make restoring a law, regulation, or policy difficult.[26] In a multicellular organism, *apoptosis* (programmed and predictable cell death) serves a similar purpose, namely that of preventing non-productive parts of the organism from consuming resources.[27]

Legal apoptosis (LA) can be most easily effected by an amendment to the federal constitution—an amendment that could easily be made to apply to every level of government, from national laws and regulations to city ordinances. America would not inevitably enter an era of lawlessness after 20 years, but each law nearing its end would need to be specifically reviewed and renewed (with no option for omnibus legislation) after going through the appropriate committee.[28]

Every federal regulation would need to complete the rulemaking process as well. Finally, all interpretations of statutes and regulations, be they at the executive level (meaning letters of clarification or executive orders) or judicial level (meaning appellate court opinions) would expire when the law or regulation upon which they are based terminates— this might well be described as *derivative death or host/ parasite death.* In the matter of judicial opinions, they would remain binding upon the instant case but would cease to serve as published legal precedent.

Were every law currently in existence to expire at the same time, the legislatures might well be overwhelmed. Thus, LA for existing statutes could be staggered throughout the first 20-year term, with no delays needed thereafter.

Keeping the Bastards Busy

The process of statutory renewal described herein would be laborious. A great deal of legislative time would be dedicated to examining and reenacting laws that are nearing their expiry. Courts would be obligated to review new statutes and interpret them afresh on an almost daily basis. Bureaucracies would be forever engaged in some part of the rulemaking process. And officials would find themselves having to rewrite memos they can but vaguely remember drafting years prior. Even law enforcement officers would need to spend a portion of their day noting what laws had been reinstated without significant modification, what laws had been changed, and what laws had been allowed to ascend to the great legal library in the sky (or descend to the great legal library of the depths, as the case may be). The workload for *everyone* in government would almost certainly increase, particularly during the first LA cycle, after which thousands of pages of law would cease to be more than ink and fibers to be pulped, if not more expeditiously used to remedy the permanent emergency of toilet paper shortages.

And that is the point!

Every law, regulation, binding policy, and city ordinance would require ongoing effort to sustain. This effort would be considerable: It would occupy so much of the government's time that entirely new laws would be passed infrequently and only when deemed to be worth the additional workload. Old laws—laws that were created to address an ancient crisis, real or fabricated by opportunists—would naturally pass away, as would whatever oppressive restrictions or archaic verbiage they contain.[29] Additionally, laws that serve only to facilitate the harassment and annoyance of the citizenry would simply be allowed to reach the end of their lifespan, with few legislators willing to sponsor, time and again, laws known only for infuriating constituents and frustrating their peace of mind and quiet enjoyment of life.

Finally, there is the matter of legal precedence and case law. Since *Marbury v. Madison,* the United States Supreme Court has served as much as a decider of law as of cases, with its influence and ability to effectively *construct* law from the bench growing more powerful over the generations. Court-ordered school desegregation,[30] the right to an abortion,[31] and the right to same-sex marriage[32]—even those who most ardently support rights and obligations developed by the Court will find that a close reading of the Constitution and relevant Court decisions reveals little in the way of textual or historical support for said judicial fabrications.

There is no reason to presume that any of these court-crafted rights and duties would need to die by way of LA when the cases upon which they were established expire. Rather, they could be incorporated into perpetually revised and modernized statutes.

And those rights that people truly hold dear and believe should be woven into the fabric of the law can be further assured of permanence by way of new amendments to the federal constitution, establishing for them a degree of nearly irrevocable recognition that no Supreme Court decision can offer. Our confusion as to *what means what* can be lessened, when we no longer need to rely upon the courts—at best, nine noble (if completely unaccountable to the public) lawyer-scholars, at worst, *an assortment of assholes and cunts*—to determine how language more than two centuries old should be applied in the smartphone age.[33]

What Shall Remain? What Problems Are Likely to Arise?

In the civilian world, only the state and federal constitutions—nothing else. These foundational documents of government should endure for a longer time than statutes, although even they may need to be given expiration dates of no more than a few generations. As for the armed forces, their operation is so different from that of the civilian world that the Uniform Code of Military Justice and the code of the Last Chance Corps (assuming the LCC is ever established) might well need to have longer lifespans than would ordinary law.

As for additional problems, the most probable is that certain legislatures may attempt to circumvent these time limitations by incorporating statutes into their respective state constitutions. (The federal amendment process would make doing this somewhat more difficult.) One need not speculate that this *could happen*, as it already has. The Constitution of the State of Alabama runs more than 300,000 words and has more than 900 amendments,[34] making it less of a document detailing the rights of the people and the essential functions of the government, than a legal code—one addressing everything from the elimination of boll weevils[35] to the promotion of the catfish industry[36]—structured as a series of amendments. The solution to this problem is for the courts (or a designated oversight body) to identify purely statutory amendments and assign them the same lifespan as state code.

The last problem worth noting is that of legislatures endeavoring to periodically revive plainly unconstitutional laws (race-based voting restrictions, etc.). There is no perfect remedy for this. The reintroduction of the exact text of an already unconstitutional statute might well be forbidden by a dedicated amendment to the federal constitution, but even the dimmest of dimwits can figure out how to change around a word or two with the help of a thesaurus.

The courts might well need to relitigate nearly identical constitutional issues, but this would stand to keep both appellate courts appropriately busy and disincline them from attempting to reach too far and justify their existences by pulling new rights and duties from the thinnest of judicial air.

Memento Mori

To every thing there is a season, and a time to every purpose under the heaven . . . —Ecclesiastes 3:1

There is no eternal law. The Code of Hammurabi, the Law of Moses, the Draconian constitution—all these, no matter how great and wise they were for their day, are no more suited to the modern world than would be the best metalsmithing techniques of the Bronze Age. The inevitability of death—for law, for people, for conventions—serves to temper the ego, not just of the man, but of the institution. And death itself skims off the dross of fads and momentary panics. There are undeniable benefits to knowing that a cold and merciless hand shall someday tear the light and warmth of existence from the bosom of every man, beast, and human creation—those of encouraging examination and reflection and reminding us that our time is dearly limited.

As it is with men, so it should be with the laws of mankind.

151

Illusion, Delusion, and Empire

The last 600 years—the totality of modern history—were an invention of the West. Art, industry, law, music, philosophy, science, and technology—there was no field of consequence we did not dominate. From Shakespeare, Beethoven, and Nietzsche to Newton, Poincaré, and Watson and Crick, almost every thinker and doer of note was a product of Western schools, families, and genius. And the few who were not— Satyendra Nath Bose (of the Bose-Einstein condensate), for one—were largely educated in the European tradition.[1] Apart from Japan's appearance on the world stage during the Meiji Restoration (with an attendant victory in the Russo-Japanese War)[2] and her post-WWII development into a powerhouse of technological development, there were no major challenges to Euro-American hegemony until the concluding few decades of the 20th century.

Then things changed. Korea rose, establishing that one neither need be of European descent nor Japanese to build a decent microwave oven.[3] The Chinese proved that they could make anything (with foreign guidance). And the Portuguese empire, which began in 1415, ended with the handover of Macau to the People's Republic.[4] Such was the closing of an era.

Still, we could maintain our claims of unquestionable preeminence. They might be weaker than they were in our days of wine and roses, but there was no one ready to replace us, and after the fall of the Soviet Union, nothing to impede us. America might not have colonies, but she garrisoned the globe,[5] and extraordinary air power had served the national interest well since the storied days of General Curtis LeMay.[6]

Even the attacks of September 11 did less to undermine Americans' faith in occidental supremacy than to reinforce the idea that America *could win*—could impose democracy, peace, capitalism, and socially progressive ideals upon the target of our choice—if she but took off her gloves. Take them off she did. If the 1990s were the age of *irrational exuberance* for the financial markets, the 2000s were one of similar enthusiasm for the surveillance state, the special operative, the torturer, and the warfighter.[7]

And that brings us to the present—2021—the withdrawal from Afghanistan is complete. The government we built and subsidized did not last long enough to wave goodbye to us. When Britain departed India, the language, courts, and bureaucracy remained. When Portugal returned Macau, casinos, Catholicism, and tapas hung back. And when the French abandoned Vietnam, baguettes and coffee stood strong with the people.

What of Afghanistan? What have we left there? What remains but craters, toxic detritus, and arms? This—the absolute failure of the West's final attempt at imperialism—is the most significant event in centuries. It shows what we cannot do. It elucidates what we cannot change and whom we cannot influence.

We abandoned our bases in the night. We packed up, turned off the lights, and flew home.[8] Victors do not do this. They do not forsake their accomplishments as easily as that.

What of the future? *Our long 2020* may well not end until 2035. By then, every major advantage the West has will almost certainly be matched by another people, if not many other peoples.[9] This is wonderful. This is the best of news.

Now, we need care for no one else. The empire is dead. Even the illusion of empire has shattered. Our elite will delude themselves for some time still. Let them. Feed their idiocy, cultivate it, and turn it against them. They are a blight. The universe needs no masters, and billions of lives will improve once these masters are gone.

We opened this book with Fortune, our dear trickster. We end it with her as well. She long fools only the willfully fooled. As for the rest of us, we must know this: These are good times, and they are getting better, despite protestations to the contrary.

Because these are the best years ever.

Notes
Best Year Ever

(1) For those who do not get the joke: Sir Thomas More was decapitated.
See https://tinyurl.com/y7pj6s6z

(2) The Buddhist concept of *conditioned things*:
See https://tinyurl.com/edc2kk65

(3) Dead convicts and road trips! Hooray!
See https://tinyurl.com/4bfyfzjc

(4) *The End of History* is both a concept and a book. The short explanation: The liberal democratic order would prevail across the world, with much prosperity and peace resulting thereof.
See https://tinyurl.com/yz8mdph9

(5) The Saudi government funds the teaching of *Wahhabism*—one of the most conservative (and anti-Western) schools of Islam—by building schools and mosques around the world.
See https://tinyurl.com/6fvuxj74

(6) For the young'uns: In the 1980s, the United States sold weapons to Iran (an enemy at the time) so that it could subsidize *the Contras*—anti-communist rebels in Nicaragua. As is often the case with U.S.-backed fighters, the Contras were not the kindest and gentlest of people. They were known for widespread torture and execution of civilians. By supporting this group (or so the reasoning went) the United States could promote *freedom and human rights*. And proving that old habits die hard, the United States is funding the group once again. *Why?* Your guess is as good as mine.
See https://tinyurl.com/bvwdjn4c

(7) The Manhattan Project relied heavily on imported brainpower.
See https://tinyurl.com/5apddy7v

(8) The U.S. has the world's highest incarceration rate.
See https://tinyurl.com/h7dw8kx2

(9) Transfer of materiel to law enforcement happened under Program 1033.
See https://tinyurl.com/r96jw74

(10) Not only goatherds are killed, but also any number of poor schlubs at the wrong place at the wrong time.
See https://tinyurl.com/4kamy6ep

(11) I am as capitalistic as they come, but after listening to the Soviet anthem, even I want to collectivize something.
Hear https://tinyurl.com/2me5ydnc

(12) Apparently, some people do not like being bombed. *Who knew?*
See https://tinyurl.com/f5kesev5

(13) Yes, Hillary Clinton did refer to *superpredators*, and yes, she was fearmongering. She was not the first to do this. She will not be the last. Politicians manipulate us with fear *because we let them.*
See https://tinyurl.com/3ejx3hwa

(14) Yet more fearmongering, *sleeper cells* (as a concept) were borrowed from anti-communist propaganda. Finding any real ones has proven difficult.
See https://tinyurl.com/2av3r3kp

(15) A) Probably the biggest non-event in decades, Y2K was supposed to hit underprepared nations, such as China, particularly hard. Yet almost no problems were reported, even there.
See https://tinyurl.com/f6n3bsdc
B) No major problems in China.
See https://tinyurl.com/devvfkxy
C) A general summary of events:
See https://tinyurl.com/puvxwnb8

(16) Asian giant hornets are also called *murder hornets*—a hyperbolic term for an insect, but a great name for a football team.
See https://tinyurl.com/afvkexe7

(17) One could take the Global War on Terror as a never-ending money pit, but a smaller and better-documented example is the development of the Federal Bureau of Investigation's Virtual Case File program.
See https://tinyurl.com/4msfuye6

(18) We have less choice in media than we realize, with many different media brands being controlled by a handful of companies.
See https://tinyurl.com/tazb347z

(19) Distrust of experts is an American tradition. We've just gotten better at it.
See https://tinyurl.com/nfrjw8by

(20) Predictions as to the effects of COVID and predictions as to the effects of reopening the economy have been dramatic, confusing, and alarmist. This is the result of structural flaws in the United States public health system and competing political agendas.
See https://tinyurl.com/4597n969

(21) I am not suggesting that COVID-19 is a hoax. The evidence that it is a real virus that can cause real harm is considerable. What I *am* stating is that the institutional response to the spread of the disease was both excessive and inconsistent. Certainly, some safety measures and precautions should have been taken, but they should have been more focused on protecting uniquely vulnerable populations, such as the elderly and those with compromised immune systems.

(22) A) Defining American values can be difficult, largely because Americans emphasize individualism so much that they hesitate to make statements about the collective. Nevertheless, researchers developed a list of 13 values widely shared by Americans.
See https://tinyurl.com/vhspvmyv
B) These are far from universal. One of these (Item 3 on the list) is the belief that meeting deadlines is more important than taking the time to build relationships. This indicates a

monochronic culture. The differences between such cultures and their opposite (*polychronic* cultures) have been the subject of much study.
See https://tinyurl.com/tsand6dm

(23) A) One could also argue that the Iraq War served to enrich defense contractors, but that could be said about every conflict since the age of Smedley D. Butler (and probably a great many before then).
See https://tinyurl.com/e7mk23pt
and https://tinyurl.com/5fbsz64z
B) As for the reasons for the war, true believers in *the American Way* (largely neoconservatives) played a role in initiating it.
See https://tinyurl.com/dcyujsmz
C) Other writers have examined this assertion that the Iraq War was not about oil in more depth than I could.
See https://tinyurl.com/n7zx6bv2

(24) This tendency to remain isolated from the local population is not unique to Americans abroad. Foreign students in United States college rarely know their American classmates well, with language limitations explaining some of this social disconnect.
See https://tinyurl.com/46hemthc
and https://tinyurl.com/4uve94jr

(25) A) There is no entirely objective way to quantify provincialism. Generally, Americans do not travel much.
See https://tinyurl.com/2c25ew79
B) As for the elite, most college graduates do not travel, and of those who do, the majority travel to Europe, rather than regions with greater cultural differences.
See https://tinyurl.com/4hb793tr

(26) Dunning-Kruger effect:
See https://tinyurl.com/3c7xd5m5

(27) Even the annoyingly human-rights concerned Europeans are not without their sins, and not just in their brutal exploitation of non-European peoples throughout the colonial era.

See https://tinyurl.com/5b9etst5

(28) While writing this, I thought of Michigan, where I studied for several years.
See https://tinyurl.com/2nxpwwy4
and https://tinyurl.com/d3h5nmut

(29) The world views America differently than it did a few years ago. The simplistic argument (as follows) blames Trump almost exclusively, but there is almost certainly more to it than that. One diplomat's take on the matter summarized the major points.
See https://tinyurl.com/4zweh47h

(30) This fine phrase was borrowed, slightly modified, from C.S. Lewis.
See https://tinyurl.com/2phxzf3s

(31) A) We take for granted that Chinese values (and Eastern values in general) are different from those of the West; however, that is not to say that most of us have a clear understanding of them. For a detailed analysis of said Chinese values (to be compared to the survey and review of American values referenced in Note 22):
See https://tinyurl.com/4s9ayaa3
B) For a Chinese perspective of the Middle Kingdom's role in world history see *Superpower Interrupted: The Chinese History of the World*.

(32) The United States has a total of 234 active-duty bases, 66 of which are overseas. The total cost of Base Operation Support (BOS), which only covers the essentials of keeping the base itself functional, not the cost of weaponry, et cetera, was $25 billion in 2016, with the cost of maintaining a single overseas base being much higher than that of maintaining one in the United States.
See https://tinyurl.com/2znxxypy

(33) Most children can grasp the rudiments of the scientific method. At least one video explains the fundamentals in language a ten-year-old child should be able to understand.

See https://tinyurl.com/69jb9se3

(34) A) Not everyone with the title of *scientist* follows the scientific method, hence Lysenko and his bizarre notions (and keep in mind that he was regarded as a much-respected *expert* for much of his life).
See https://tinyurl.com/kk83nmu3
B) Most of Lysenko's experimental results could not be replicated, and *replicability* is the hallmark of good science. Much of modern social *science* suffers from the same problem.
See https://tinyurl.com/3kykyrbc

(35) Bernays and his significance will be explored more later in this essay. Read about him.
See https://tinyurl.com/a86ejjnt

(36) See https://tinyurl.com/wbdwxnfk

(37) See https://tinyurl.com/454v47s7

(38) A) Murder rates have varied throughout American history, but even at their highest, they are estimated to have never exceeded 35/100,000—considerable, but not unimaginably so. And by 1800, they were below 20/100,000.
See https://tinyurl.com/455xke6d
And these rates never approached the horrific number of premature deaths that happened during WWI, WWII, or any number of cultural upheavals and revolutions.
B) Going back further in history is difficult. Statistics were not gathered with any consistency before the 19th century, but several estimates of historical homicide rates exist. The most violent years in Europe were around 1450, with national homicide rates ranging from 73/100,000 (in Italy) to 16/100,000 (Germany and Switzerland). Both numbers are elevated by modern standards, but they are far below the levels one associates with social chaos.
See https://tinyurl.com/4fmtj6hf

(39) If current demographic trends continue in America, Whites will become a minority by around 2045.
See https://tinyurl.com/bz4d92jy

(40) Obviously, there is an element of prediction to this statement, but what *is* certain is that Millennials are poorer than their parents were at the same age.
See https://tinyurl.com/4ccdn72f

(41) A) Again, I am making a prediction, but this is based on solid evidence. First, non-Asian minorities are poorer than Whites (on average).
See https://tinyurl.com/2x2sk2h7
B) Next, there is the matter of minorities being less trusting of authorities. Blacks typically hold the police in lower regard than do Whites (perhaps with good reason).
See https://tinyurl.com/88x7ah8r

(42) This phrase—*hombres armados*—is taken from a movie, *Men with Guns* being the English-language title. I am not suggesting that *no one* should ever trust the police, but *blind* trust in authority is hardly a sign of wisdom or maturity.

(43) A) Research on the effects of body cam footage suggests that the technology has mixed results on officer behavior.
See https://tinyurl.com/md9z2pwb
B) However, this is still an emerging technology, and its effects may take some time to be felt. One would have a difficult time imagining the current George Floyd protests taking place without video evidence of exactly what happened.

(44) Occasionally, a judge makes such an ass of himself (or herself) that a public outcry ensues. Such would be unlikely were the proceedings not recorded. For an example of a judge who became video infamous:
See https://tinyurl.com/mduz8x7r

(45) This closely relates to the concept of *compassion fade*.
See https://tinyurl.com/w24chr5a

(46) One may argue that there were some legitimate grounds for the University of Missouri protests (largely relating to medical insurance for graduate students); however, the same cannot be said about Occupy Wall Street—a movement/political action so poorly defined that almost no one, protestors

included, knew what the protests were supposed to achieve. Gaining a bit of insight into the well-meaning (and sometimes amusing) befuddlement of protestors is worth the effort.
See https://tinyurl.com/yuzwhz8t

(47) A) Even the community of journalists could not excuse the sheer reckless behavior of Sabrina Rubin Erdely, the author of "A Rape on Campus."
See https://tinyurl.com/2tdd8677
B) The Kavanaugh hearings were based on largely incoherent accusations.
See https://tinyurl.com/wk9m54ub
C) Finally, #MeToo, while possibly well-intentioned at the beginning (or not, who knows?) degenerated into something so vitriolic that even some feminists found it suspect.
See https://tinyurl.com/8ny5kadt
D) As for the command to care, what effect would any of these movements/claims have were more of us simply to declare "I do not care!"?

(48) And those who are *too* performative in their politically correct Madam Mao-approved playacting, are subject to public criticism as well.
See https://tinyurl.com/mbhe3746

(49) For more information on how to be a better bastard, read "On Being a Bastard" in my book.
See https://tinyurl.com/py6m474y

(50) The Chinese Cultural Revolution demanded millions of apologies from at least as many supposed wrongdoers, be they teachers, landed farmers, or businesspeople. One lesson to be learned from that era: Apply enough pressure and you can make most people confess to (and apologize for) just about anything, even if the allegations entail impossible claims. And the long-term effect of this—a culture of cynicism and indifference. See *The Tragedy of Liberation: A History of the Chinese Revolution 1945–1957*.

We should not underestimate the horrific cruelty that lies in the hearts of many. Nothing brings this badness out faster than shows of weakness, which is why complying with those who demand confessions and apologies oftentimes does little but make them angrier.

(51) See https://tinyurl.com/2s3tb5mn

(52) This school is still in business, and it offers some classes in English.
See https://tinyurl.com/ajdv2s64

(53) See https://tinyurl.com/uusaj8s

(54) See https://tinyurl.com/4hjpm84a

(55) Although many people can benefit from vocational training, a smaller number have the cognitive capacity to benefit from college.
See https://tinyurl.com/4bmn86u5
and https://tinyurl.com/5fbfrvzv

(56) A) Hyperactivity (ADHD) is overdiagnosed.
See https://tinyurl.com/2md7aub5
B) Autism is likely overdiagnosed as well.
See https://tinyurl.com/2c2hb3mh
C) Efforts to categorize bad behavior or beliefs go back years, to when *racism* started to be seen as both the result and the cause of a medical or mental problem, rather than simply being a belief or part of an unpleasant disposition.
See https://tinyurl.com/y9bctxm7
D) Finally there is the matter of student loans. How bad are they?
See https://tinyurl.com/rku6ahhc

(57) Love fades, but hate is eternal. Ellison knew this well.
See https://tinyurl.com/ydux69hh

(58) See https://tinyurl.com/4re49jz5

(59) For an explanation of *tacit knowledge*:
See https://tinyurl.com/yenmdf6y

(60) The cost of sponsoring a worker under the H-1B visa program ranges from a few thousand dollars to much more. See https://tinyurl.com/4595s2rw

(61) See https://tinyurl.com/m2cjahz6

(62) A great deal of formal schooling does little more than serve as an economic signaling mechanism. See *The Case against Education: Why the Education System Is a Waste of Time and Money.*

(63) How long colleges can afford to sponsor sports teams is uncertain. Stanford University—with some of the best athletic teams in the United States—is cutting 11 teams. Granted, neither basketball nor football was on the chopping block, but for a school of Stanford's size to cut so many teams is significant.
See https://tinyurl.com/yjf7k4rw

(64) A) University publishing houses have not fared well during COVID. They will need to either adapt or die.
See https://tinyurl.com/duuv2sj4
B) Academic research laboratories were largely closed as well.
See https://tinyurl.com/5d7buudm

(65) Employers began to rely more heavily on college education as a sorting tool for prospective workers after other assessment tools were largely banned under *Griggs v. Duke Power Company.*
See https://tinyurl.com/n65e5byu

(66) Regarding classic literature: Project Gutenberg provides thousands of texts at no cost, and a great many lectures from esteemed professors can be found online as well. MIT's program is just one of many.
See https://tinyurl.com/cduepuf8

(67) If anything, instruction in the humanities should be *less* regulated than that in the martial arts: Flimflam academies of postmodern literature are far less dangerous to their students than are Frank Dux-style *Con Kwon Do* schools. When was the

164

last time anyone thought a working knowledge of Derrida would save him from an ass beating in a street fight? Although I suspect a great many of my readers have already seen his footage, YouTuber Joe Rogan has much fun tearing apart fake martial arts.
See https://tinyurl.com/y7z779k9

(68) Intelligence is a fragile trait, and without aggressive selection pressures, it is subject to rapid decay.
See https://tinyurl.com/b3yet9ap

(69) A) Most Americans do not know their neighbors.
See https://tinyurl.com/44jnn9pk
B) More generally, we have become increasingly isolated over the last few decades, although such does not necessarily bother us.
See https://tinyurl.com/3yzvy5bs
and https://tinyurl.com/yn55dfkw

(70) A) The first welding robot was developed in the 1960s.
See https://tinyurl.com/sycuc7mn
B) The first surgical robot was developed in the 1980s.
See https://tinyurl.com/v6t577hx

(71) A) A brief history of the DARPA Grand Challenge.
See https://tinyurl.com/y7wuhuf6
B) Tesla's recent advancements in self-driving technology.
See https://tinyurl.com/9b56w9za

(72) Walmart relies more on robots now than it did even a few years ago, and it will deploy even more in the coming years.
See https://tinyurl.com/37e26fzz

(73) *Fight for 15* started in New York, and it has expanded to many other cities.
See https://tinyurl.com/prnuzdz8

(74) Viruses may come and go, but miserable summertime heat is predictable, particularly for those working at Amazon.com's warehouses.
See https://tinyurl.com/exn6hxme

(75) See https://tinyurl.com/52xvmj4j

(76) Working from home is here to stay.
See https://tinyurl.com/2mcsy5wb
and https://tinyurl.com/8vn5wvx5
and https://tinyurl.com/2uh9fz77

(77) The Millennial preference for staying at home predates COVID.
See https://tinyurl.com/2nemb38v

(78) Staying at home is good for America. Good for us!
See https://tinyurl.com/vz7pkx9a

(79) There seems to be little research on how America has historically regarded those who prefer to be by themselves. Still, the benefits of being alone are gradually gaining recognition.
See https://tinyurl.com/2nds6enp

(80) A) Total gasoline consumption for 2019.
See https://tinyurl.com/twbwxac9
B) Number of miles driven per person (2018).
See https://tinyurl.com/22yhmak
The numbers are not for the *same* year, but they are within one year of each. *Good enough is good enough!*

(81) A) There were more than 30,000 vehicular deaths in 2019.
See https://tinyurl.com/fpucu9bt
B) Since the COVID pandemic, insurance claims for accidents have dropped 50%.
See https://tinyurl.com/pmzyshdw
Thus, fewer miles driven should lead to fewer accidents and lost lives.

(82) Commute times have been getting worse for decades in the United States. This article refers to 9 *calendar days*, which is about the same amount of time as in *19 workdays*.
See https://tinyurl.com/smz7avku
and https://tinyurl.com/5fz4h3z5

(83) Meetings waste time and money.
See https://tinyurl.com/27mr66z2

(84) The average office worker spends 2.5 hours per day on emails. A truly skilled time killer can spend far more!
See https://tinyurl.com/xr98j7r6

(85) Telegrams were remarkably short by modern messaging standards, with the shortest known being sent by Oscar Wilde to his publisher. Living in France at the time, Wilde wanted to know how well one of his books was selling. The message he sent consisted of a single character—?—his publisher's reply: *!*
See https://tinyurl.com/2e8wb5wb

(86) Middle management is likely to take a post-COVID beating.
See https://tinyurl.com/rk3dbww8
There is also the matter of *flattening organizational structure*.
See https://tinyurl.com/4end49hv

(87) The low-hanging fruit hypothesis has already been developed at tremendous length. See *The Great Stagnation: How America Ate All the Low-Hanging Fruit of Modern History, Got Sick, and Will (Eventually) Feel Better.*

(88) Psychology is just one domain in which old studies would never gain modern approval.
See https://tinyurl.com/3recky93

(89) The first airplane death.
See https://tinyurl.com/yfcyaj7z

(90) A) Disastrously dangerous radiation experiments.
See https://tinyurl.com/2dmh6wsh
B) The first dog in space was essentially cooked alive.
See https://tinyurl.com/uf2euack

(91) A) Lightning-fast genome sequencing of COVID.
See https://tinyurl.com/3svyp3np
B) And equally speedy vaccine development.
See https://tinyurl.com/4s3xma2u
C) Innovation in other domains is speeding up as well.
See https://tinyurl.com/3sdyys2y

(92) The law school I attended during the pandemic (and from which I recently graduated) moved from in-person classes to online classes in three days. Other schools did the same.
See https://tinyurl.com/tae9xppt

(93) Courts around the world are learning the benefits of Zoom.
See https://tinyurl.com/yp9b9sux

(94) The *New York Times* offered an extraordinarily biased interpretation of the article.
See https://tinyurl.com/23sxz7cw
The original paper is more interesting.
See https://tinyurl.com/ytfc2v9c

(95) A) Free trade benefits the rich everywhere and the poor in the developing world. In the developed world, it leads to "polarization in local wages, employment, skill attainment, and individual welfare," which is another way of saying that it tends to make the rich richer and the poor poorer—not a great thing for the middle class.
See https://tinyurl.com/83vmndns
B) Obviously, this harm was not exclusive to the Black family, but a great many Black families did depend on the solid factory work and wages that allowed them to climb out of poverty, earning far more than they could have in the South.
See https://tinyurl.com/scwz5fdf
C) As for those who would blame free trade on those evil Republicans, note that it was a decidedly bipartisan effort—the elites on both sides of the aisle did all in their power to rob the American worker of opportunity. Consider the history of the (recently renegotiated) North American Free Trade Agreement (NAFTA).
See https://tinyurl.com/8raurup3
D) As for social welfare, how does it undermine the family? Let us count the many ways.
See https://tinyurl.com/fjmhd5um
and https://tinyurl.com/3z752hds
and https://tinyurl.com/yr4nfh6a

Establishing a perfect causal relationship between social welfare and Black family destruction is difficult, but that is a problem common to almost any matter investigated by the social sciences.

(96) A) The effects of the gentrification of the New York City area are well known.
See https://tinyurl.com/rz7nkjvr
B) And violent crime has dropped a great deal in the City, which is not to say that there are not plenty of crooks.
See https://tinyurl.com/pdb58jdr

(97) A) Solitude is one thing, extreme forced isolation is another, and its effects can be measurably severe. They include greatly increased aggression and fear.
See https://tinyurl.com/efss49sm
B) I explore this topic further in "The Dark Forest: Recognizing the Naturalness of Misandry and Misanthropy" of *The Rules* (page 219).
See https://tinyurl.com/2crrbu9e

(98) I am using food and starvation as a metaphor, but the metaphor is grounded in fact.
See https://tinyurl.com/ncxkw9n5

(99) See https://tinyurl.com/yuyrs6ew

(100) The sexual revolution almost certainly undermined family and (by extension) community, which in turn led to the growth of identity politics. *Primal Screams: How the Sexual Revolution Created Identity Politics* addresses this hypothesis in considerable (and fascinating) detail.
Unfortunately, extremist ideologies do not so much cure the problem of societal disconnect as they do weaponize it. And given time, a great many ideologies either collapse under the weight of their radicals or become self-parodying.

(101) Academic life can be surprisingly stressful.
See https://tinyurl.com/ybzbvb2k
and https://tinyurl.com/3frr26bm

(102) See Note 94, *New York Times* link. The *NYT* article contains the phrase "should be burned to the ground" (without referring to atomic conflagration). How this should be taken is up for debate. I suspect that some survey respondents meant this literally. Others might have had destruction of a more metaphorical sort in mind. Either way, this does not bode well for many. If a fourth of the population sees little in America worth preserving, those with much to lose have much to fear.

(103) *Notes from Underground* was published in 1864, not long after the end of the Crimean War and during the middle of Alexander II's economic and legal reforms.
See https://tinyurl.com/9fjmaf

(104) Although I have briefly referenced the matter of isolation in academia previously (Note 101), here is more evidence of the isolation of academics and how it stands to harm them.
See https://tinyurl.com/yh3p2ru5
and https://tinyurl.com/pyvem9p4

(105) And herein lies the great contradiction in American society: On a theoretical level, we advocate a radical form of self-development that rises to the level of Nietzschean *master morality*—something that Nietzsche would almost certainly attack as impractical for the greater part of humanity to achieve. On a practical level, we promote an engineered, conformist culture created by teams of marketers (and increasingly, computers). The sentence associated with this endnote is a paraphrase of an Edward Bernays' quote.
See https://tinyurl.com/4u4xr5er

(106) See https://tinyurl.com/ktv6tsyw

(107) Life goes on, and it continues with less change than one might think.
See https://tinyurl.com/ur2ktj4n

(108) *The World of Yesterday* is well worth reading.

(109) Exactly when the Chinese fell behind the West is uncertain, but that it happened during the time of Manchu (Qing) governance is almost certainly beyond doubt.
See https://tinyurl.com/6pkernvr
and https://tinyurl.com/upf3947f

(110) The cost of our 21st-century military adventures is astounding.
See https://tinyurl.com/mhpxbrxp

(111) A) American medical costs are the highest of any country.
See https://tinyurl.com/7yn284wc
B) Among the many things that COVID did was drive home the fact that not everyone will be able to receive unlimited care when resources grow scarce, hence the ongoing debate over who gets a ventilator.
See https://tinyurl.com/3suv8yty
C) This discussion should have started *years* earlier, with one writer, Sheri Fink, having considered this some depth in *Five Days at Memorial: Life and Death in a Storm-Ravaged* Hospital, her book about a crisis at a New Orleans hospital during Hurricane Katrina. Either way, better late than never!

(112) As much as I wish I could take credit for the observation that the Industrial Revolution/Long 19th Century was a singularity of sorts, I cannot.
See https://tinyurl.com/yvk9a3bh

Avoiding Thucydides's Trap

(1) See https://tinyurl.com/4zr9bx3u

(2) See https://tinyurl.com/a8mddxar

(3) See https://tinyurl.com/vyueuj3u

(4) See https://tinyurl.com/4tyxtn6m

(5) See https://tinyurl.com/f2remzt5

(6) See https://tinyurl.com/m7234uav

(7) See https://tinyurl.com/53xxjj73

(8) See https://tinyurl.com/4tm64ts6

(9) See https://tinyurl.com/4trfxvma

(10) See https://tinyurl.com/3pzv65fw

(11) See https://tinyurl.com/xtbnkuxv

(12) See https://tinyurl.com/n3u28dd8

(13) See https://tinyurl.com/44new5d4

(14) See https://tinyurl.com/5eabk4yf

(15) See https://tinyurl.com/jefzzdtw

(16) See https://tinyurl.com/ys5ate44

(17) See https://tinyurl.com/3tcyy8k4

(18) See https://tinyurl.com/4dfyu7z6

(19) See https://tinyurl.com/hvv64ffm

(20) See https://tinyurl.com/3mzp4ru6

(21) See https://tinyurl.com/3ynnpf3j

(22) See https://tinyurl.com/vumk5nkz

(23) See https://tinyurl.com/d5km7hp6

(24) See https://tinyurl.com/a65dv25w

(25) See https://tinyurl.com/5ewpsk7s

(26) See https://tinyurl.com/3tm3cdtn

(27) See https://tinyurl.com/7mjfvnfc

(28) See https://tinyurl.com/7k9x93tp

(29) See https://tinyurl.com/8u8ms4jh

(30) See https://tinyurl.com/hbhwe6z7

(31) See https://tinyurl.com/4e5hxz48

(32) See https://tinyurl.com/yvd36ttr

(33) See https://tinyurl.com/3b3z7tvy

(34) See https://tinyurl.com/4t6252zw

(35) See https://tinyurl.com/m3zk537p

(36) See https://tinyurl.com/rrr67d9u

(37) See https://tinyurl.com/k4jnhw8m

(38) See https://tinyurl.com/xb69fkxz

(39) See https://tinyurl.com/x957vvty

(40) See https://tinyurl.com/uuuav7cw

(41) See https://tinyurl.com/bdbrr4m6

(42) See https://tinyurl.com/2fxusmn2

(43) See https://tinyurl.com/dnnu2zbp

(44) See https://tinyurl.com/rr3eepxr

(45) See https://tinyurl.com/4w5bhu87

(46) See https://tinyurl.com/4wy7ba8y

(47) See https://tinyurl.com/4h8ppxa6

(48) See https://tinyurl.com/a3v4t296

(49) See https://tinyurl.com/59spwayf

(50) See https://tinyurl.com/355p54xu

(51) See https://tinyurl.com/dcbfpzxc

(52) See https://tinyurl.com/5fnuz3pr

(53) See https://tinyurl.com/wsz2e4kn

(54) See https://tinyurl.com/2wxwwhn8

(55) See https://tinyurl.com/24exsbwx

(56) See https://tinyurl.com/4sbpvu9v

(57) See https://tinyurl.com/ubtbxbvh

(58) See https://tinyurl.com/wxu22u7m

(59) See https://tinyurl.com/ywh8uvew

(60) See https://tinyurl.com/ysy6kcf4

(61) See https://tinyurl.com/cy7ts6m4

(62) See https://tinyurl.com/a5pmz6ut

(63) See https://tinyurl.com/6sayxv9n

(64) See https://tinyurl.com/smkytm83

(65) See https://tinyurl.com/fe57sv32

(66) See https://tinyurl.com/6ydynust

(67) See https://tinyurl.com/ahdyn5ev

(68) See https://tinyurl.com/7hdamcxb

(69) See https://tinyurl.com/8rpp8hej

(70) See https://tinyurl.com/5h5bd2h4

(71) See https://tinyurl.com/y37s838r

(72) See https://tinyurl.com/3jmemym7

(73) See https://tinyurl.com/2fhrcmfw

(74) See https://tinyurl.com/v6326vjm

(75) See https://tinyurl.com/rb623x4p

(76) See https://tinyurl.com/jzcpe68

(77) See https://tinyurl.com/zjuc533r

(78) See https://tinyurl.com/4mb7ak3p

(79) See https://tinyurl.com/9axh8f7d

(80) See https://tinyurl.com/587nm69s

(81) See https://tinyurl.com/5yr5jdwz

(82) See https://tinyurl.com/d46dahdc

(83) See https://tinyurl.com/ymrpwe8y

(84) See https://tinyurl.com/55bz2y3x

(85) See https://tinyurl.com/ezrrjab5

(86) See https://tinyurl.com/fw57em

(87) See https://tinyurl.com/m7k4d4pu

(88) See https://tinyurl.com/92upbrx9

(89) See https://tinyurl.com/24x5t44w

(90) See https://tinyurl.com/3yp6ecc8

(91) See https://tinyurl.com/yxe9ebwj

(92) See https://tinyurl.com/jzdnpwyh

(93) See https://tinyurl.com/pcwut8zu

(94) See https://tinyurl.com/3drzv92n

(95) See https://tinyurl.com/2s8fuw72

(96) See https://tinyurl.com/32yh7zdh

(97) See https://tinyurl.com/jy9pcx38

(98) See https://tinyurl.com/c3bp2t2r

(99) See https://tinyurl.com/vzt7uxfj

(100) See https://tinyurl.com/8yx6y5w

(101) See https://tinyurl.com/3ph3368k

(102) See https://tinyurl.com/dtzmz9rh

(103) See https://tinyurl.com/2wed6wxz

(104) See https://tinyurl.com/7eamna2h

(105) See https://tinyurl.com/3pref3y2

(106) See https://tinyurl.com/7y27e8u2

(107) See https://tinyurl.com/ydsjyrjz

(108) See https://tinyurl.com/2tvwbu74

(109) See https://tinyurl.com/59a8twfj

(110) See https://tinyurl.com/2e28tcpb

(111) See https://tinyurl.com/yjda2pct

(112) See https://tinyurl.com/2e7zpp3e

(113) See https://tinyurl.com/sp4nf7s3

(114) See https://tinyurl.com/yc4h2jmy

(115) See https://tinyurl.com/sw53nkc8

(116) See https://tinyurl.com/4ve2w4wy

(117) See https://tinyurl.com/3eetz3ru

(118) See https://tinyurl.com/hwv675z6

(119) See https://tinyurl.com/3jnpzman

(120) See https://tinyurl.com/fm6h2h6

(121) See https://tinyurl.com/3z3tky7r

(122) See https://tinyurl.com/mrjtec6u

(123) See https://tinyurl.com/3nncmvev

(124) See https://tinyurl.com/cr2mkku9

(125) See https://tinyurl.com/t3jkz5kw

(126) See https://tinyurl.com/3rwsymub

(127) See https://tinyurl.com/e74ye44r

(128) See https://tinyurl.com/4ryxx6jk

(129) See https://tinyurl.com/u7nvew3z

(130) See https://tinyurl.com/v3v59652

(131) See https://tinyurl.com/8uf4bf9s

(132) See https://tinyurl.com/3234nmmw

(133) See https://tinyurl.com/55wvhcyn

(134) See https://tinyurl.com/bvtj454b

(135) See https://tinyurl.com/ux7b7jfv

(136) See https://tinyurl.com/c8ky775d

(137) See https://tinyurl.com/26deufmr

(138) See https://tinyurl.com/ddyvr2j5

(139) See https://tinyurl.com/uy5zed9s

(140) See https://tinyurl.com/24ev6zub

(141) See https://tinyurl.com/5dfhmwvj

(142) See https://tinyurl.com/55fssehm

(143) See https://tinyurl.com/4dufz5se

(144) See https://tinyurl.com/3arar95k

(145) See https://tinyurl.com/nx5zbhaa

(146) See https://tinyurl.com/4umhc2x2

(147) See https://tinyurl.com/yz9x5bbe

(148) See https://tinyurl.com/333spwc8

(149) See https://tinyurl.com/4zswpcy2

(150) See https://tinyurl.com/dptkc43e

(151) See https://tinyurl.com/3yvtcb93

(152) See https://tinyurl.com/33ce627z

(153) See https://tinyurl.com/476ahchs

(154) See https://tinyurl.com/eaf8dv5m

(155) See https://tinyurl.com/5828ayrz

(156) See https://tinyurl.com/2jrmrfhe

(157) See https://tinyurl.com/tr9t78s

(158) See https://tinyurl.com/4rwbuff7

(159) See https://tinyurl.com/3fndmjzx

(160) See https://tinyurl.com/yfjwkk57

(161) See https://tinyurl.com/u2nuym9e

(162) See https://tinyurl.com/a547e6y4

(163) See https://tinyurl.com/t2xem83w

(164) See https://tinyurl.com/4425td2w

(165) See https://tinyurl.com/yk84yrs2

(166) See https://tinyurl.com/4tv2xtjv

(167) See https://tinyurl.com/yapkmjpk

(168) See https://tinyurl.com/a32sf253

(169) See https://tinyurl.com/328r6dfb

(170) See https://tinyurl.com/6z8xjwws

(171) See https://tinyurl.com/ys74h5zj

(172) See https://tinyurl.com/3e3ftjf4

(173) See https://tinyurl.com/9jmfvzy8

(174) See https://tinyurl.com/32wdbk7m

(175) See https://tinyurl.com/wrk4z3k7

(176) See https://tinyurl.com/26jt46jf

(177) See https://tinyurl.com/4s5fvjhy

(178) See https://tinyurl.com/c32jbm24

(179) See https://tinyurl.com/yhp7tkwj

(180) See https://tinyurl.com/m8s2m5wh

(181) See https://tinyurl.com/56zha5za

(182) See https://tinyurl.com/rb4bsk8w

(183) See https://tinyurl.com/yspm5u6x

(184) See https://tinyurl.com/367vk77f

(185) See https://tinyurl.com/e736va8m

(186) See https://tinyurl.com/p29sycnb

(187) See https://tinyurl.com/5xxnt4wb

(188) See https://tinyurl.com/2xmj5yn3

(189) See https://tinyurl.com/5au245xz

(190) See https://tinyurl.com/6t9zfysx

(191) See https://tinyurl.com/mdryfpjb

(192) See https://tinyurl.com/4474hy6y

(193) See https://tinyurl.com/2t5mf22x

(194) See https://tinyurl.com/msmrunkr

(195) See https://tinyurl.com/p69c4p4h

(196) See https://tinyurl.com/u46creaz

(197) See https://tinyurl.com/y9ewz6fu

(198) See https://tinyurl.com/kv57u2yc

(199) See https://tinyurl.com/bxh2vyf4

(200) See https://tinyurl.com/9atctvfz

(201) See https://tinyurl.com/nnb2u2fu

(202) See https://tinyurl.com/cc2ve639

(203) See https://tinyurl.com/2ndsfk6b

(204) See https://tinyurl.com/6tvbdw7r

(205) See https://tinyurl.com/7tputxrn

(206) See https://tinyurl.com/yde67maw

(207) See https://tinyurl.com/37e2h5ka

(208) See https://tinyurl.com/yjrmf4aa

(209) See https://tinyurl.com/sbeenbaj

(210) See https://tinyurl.com/4epfxzat

(211) See https://tinyurl.com/2yjnw3p

(212) See https://tinyurl.com/7e9kekmt

(213) See https://tinyurl.com/pup2v72y

(214) See https://tinyurl.com/7c5sud9m

(215) See https://tinyurl.com/79uc5hw6

(216) See https://tinyurl.com/3vtkhyhn

(217) See https://tinyurl.com/yt25t3pj

(218) See https://tinyurl.com/zxxjks2y

(219) See https://tinyurl.com/uw2upr3y

(220) See https://tinyurl.com/yfe2stym

(221) See https://tinyurl.com/ynajxwpa

(222) See https://tinyurl.com/5xz7uzz2

(223) See https://tinyurl.com/ute6jz69

(224) See https://tinyurl.com/ya56k79n

(225) See https://tinyurl.com/6rb6h76h

(226) See https://tinyurl.com/ywjpbx2r

(227) See https://tinyurl.com/fycdypky

(228) See https://tinyurl.com/2ydnrv3

(229) See https://tinyurl.com/2zkf669a

(230) See https://tinyurl.com/46sn2j4z

(231) See https://tinyurl.com/arenzun7

(232) See https://tinyurl.com/2jab9h3h

(233) See https://tinyurl.com/nrcz6ts8

(234) See https://tinyurl.com/25bwr5vw

(235) See https://tinyurl.com/2zp4jrdf

(236) See https://tinyurl.com/yhhnfwpw

(237) See https://tinyurl.com/57sk6k6b

(238) See https://tinyurl.com/7fuvyv9v

(239) See https://tinyurl.com/mremp6ry

(240) See https://tinyurl.com/nwfatzvd

(241) See https://tinyurl.com/uc2ajvvc

(242) See https://tinyurl.com/habc3x7d

(243) See https://tinyurl.com/48z3w486

(244) See https://tinyurl.com/yedndmst

(245) See https://tinyurl.com/tun3vrd5

(246) See https://tinyurl.com/k5b3h9sr

(247) See https://tinyurl.com/39vhdmx4

(248) See https://tinyurl.com/86yrxs6w

(249) See https://tinyurl.com/yx65e3ec

(250) See https://tinyurl.com/yb4d5vhv

(251) See https://tinyurl.com/dx3ywfm5

(252) See https://tinyurl.com/r5b3nxsc

(253) See https://tinyurl.com/yvcpzhrt

(254) See https://tinyurl.com/j94wn6zu

(255) See https://tinyurl.com/5capvzbs

(256) See https://tinyurl.com/c3vv7zfs

(257) See https://tinyurl.com/6cmmjchs

(258) See https://tinyurl.com/9vw3ar98

(259) See https://tinyurl.com/bydu2hm2

(260) See https://tinyurl.com/62ntpv42

(261) See https://tinyurl.com/y7vpunhv

(262) See https://tinyurl.com/yhjxrma9

(263) See https://tinyurl.com/44t4yaxv

(264) See https://tinyurl.com/d8vx26vx

(265) See https://tinyurl.com/yexmpum4

(266) See https://tinyurl.com/bwhe85av

(267) See https://tinyurl.com/ef7428pt

(268) See https://tinyurl.com/xzez2f4

(269) See https://tinyurl.com/5jakeja3

(270) See https://tinyurl.com/2vbrtv7w

(271) See https://tinyurl.com/xvyddjh2

(272) See https://tinyurl.com/3erv8nzh

(273) See https://tinyurl.com/3tuufkr2

(274) See https://tinyurl.com/6hc33nnw

(275) See https://tinyurl.com/ctfreru5

(276) See https://tinyurl.com/3nbhs8dz

(277) See https://tinyurl.com/kms395yb

(278) See https://tinyurl.com/3ksvdk3k

(279) See https://tinyurl.com/4k32nsc3

(280) See https://tinyurl.com/uddf8jda

(281) See https://tinyurl.com/nxbjjcku

(282) See https://tinyurl.com/fpfehppv

(283) See https://tinyurl.com/2s4y5jkw

(284) See https://tinyurl.com/yv77754n

(285) See https://tinyurl.com/3avv5bbe

(286) See https://tinyurl.com/mpsxrn9p

(287) See https://tinyurl.com/emhu9ys

(288) See https://tinyurl.com/upjcmp4h

(289) See https://tinyurl.com/4sv3r9ax

(290) See https://tinyurl.com/uws2t2x4

(291) See https://tinyurl.com/3my9naxa

(292) See https://tinyurl.com/rcp2ybfs

(293) See https://tinyurl.com/984th7m3

(294) See https://tinyurl.com/7kathfex

(295) See https://tinyurl.com/d8vrhu4r

(296) See https://tinyurl.com/4xbbmh8n

(297) See https://tinyurl.com/t47964e4

(298) See https://tinyurl.com/n3zk7978

(299) See https://tinyurl.com/htnpn38

(300) See https://tinyurl.com/2bf5766e

(301) See https://tinyurl.com/2z8yj759

(302) See https://tinyurl.com/v9um93f8

(303) See https://tinyurl.com/eap4uesa

(304) See https://tinyurl.com/f3jhvhax

(305) See https://tinyurl.com/37m5w6fe

(306) See https://tinyurl.com/u6w8k5jn

(307) See https://tinyurl.com/4s8asbv7

(308) See https://tinyurl.com/7zd3euvp

(309) See https://tinyurl.com/u779znx3

(310) See https://tinyurl.com/ynh7n68z

(311) See https://tinyurl.com/h7xpyk5d

(312) See https://tinyurl.com/4hw42ec9

(313) See https://tinyurl.com/9mcpps4z

(314) See https://tinyurl.com/5c445fth

(315) See https://tinyurl.com/3x42vhwr

(316) See https://tinyurl.com/4ssahexu

(317) See https://tinyurl.com/23ajavms

(318) See https://tinyurl.com/2jx3unk3

(319) See https://tinyurl.com/vcvxht2j

(320) See https://tinyurl.com/24wbttrs

(321) See https://tinyurl.com/tm5ujbuz

(322) See https://tinyurl.com/a5yr3psc

(323) See https://tinyurl.com/45ayv3js

(324) See https://tinyurl.com/r6v2u3ak

(325) See https://tinyurl.com/3d8xwtba

(326) See https://tinyurl.com/sxmda4hx

(327) See https://tinyurl.com/4ze8mmds

(328) See https://tinyurl.com/53adfj29

(329) See https://tinyurl.com/25z57h5z

(330) See https://tinyurl.com/asvrdm3s

(331) See https://tinyurl.com/222ba8tb

(332) See https://tinyurl.com/u6nkkt9h

(333) See https://tinyurl.com/6td9nvny

(334) See https://tinyurl.com/ksuaa68t

(335) See https://tinyurl.com/ua2sk57c

(336) See https://tinyurl.com/3t8c8a93

(337) See https://tinyurl.com/d4ddyhne

(338) See https://tinyurl.com/3dhwa2sk

(339) See https://tinyurl.com/3ktfm2ss

(340) See https://tinyurl.com/2rzkxnxn

(341) See https://tinyurl.com/dxbvdurk

(342) See https://tinyurl.com/bm3h2nbc

(343) See https://tinyurl.com/ppvt5n4d

(344) See https://tinyurl.com/y9vv9fnv

(345) See https://tinyurl.com/2cvhxkeh

(346) See https://tinyurl.com/5ct58ydf

(347) See https://tinyurl.com/3jtc39xv

(348) See https://tinyurl.com/y7u9du9x

(349) See https://tinyurl.com/jd8ar8cu

(350) See https://tinyurl.com/6sa663mx

(351) See https://tinyurl.com/y2y9aj8c

(352) See https://tinyurl.com/dabevjt6

The Last Chance Corps

(1) See https://tinyurl.com/v4zkz8eh

(2) See https://tinyurl.com/sy6khdzw

(3) See https://tinyurl.com/y5xnkn7k

(4) See https://tinyurl.com/ywh8m73u

(5) See https://tinyurl.com/4jx234kb

(6) See https://tinyurl.com/2x6xzedb

(7) See https://tinyurl.com/jbw3h7d4

(8) See https://tinyurl.com/p49fuxmt

(9) See https://tinyurl.com/4jx234kb

(10) See https://tinyurl.com/3hmzz3dx

(11) See https://tinyurl.com/pdj67hrb

(12) See https://tinyurl.com/4cxu5hd3

(13) See https://tinyurl.com/hrvc4zek

(14) See https://tinyurl.com/49y4757a

(15) See https://tinyurl.com/3a3fub9a

(16) See https://tinyurl.com/52bn8uyk

(17) See https://tinyurl.com/24dxpv4b

(18) See https://tinyurl.com/23z7z84a

(19) See https://tinyurl.com/y6mhtxt5

(20) See https://tinyurl.com/2eb5bh85

The Law Must Die

(1) See https://tinyurl.com/5f5a6d5f

(2) See https://tinyurl.com/ywzt72z9

(3) See https://tinyurl.com/f2avkpcs

(4) See https://tinyurl.com/pb8f35z4

(5) See https://tinyurl.com/ut9928cs

(6) See https://tinyurl.com/adsfsv9k

(7) See https://tinyurl.com/2fc7ph7p

(8) See https://tinyurl.com/2dw59jab

(9) See https://tinyurl.com/rd964bd8

(10) See https://tinyurl.com/2betcjum

(11) See https://tinyurl.com/chvb84xd

(12) See https://tinyurl.com/c6u7r3uf

(13) See https://tinyurl.com/b3db56wn

(14) See https://tinyurl.com/n2df482r

(15) See https://tinyurl.com/beyht334

(16) See https://tinyurl.com/7teuuxjf

(17) See https://tinyurl.com/29d5tcyt

(18) See https://tinyurl.com/37nhkxb8

(19) See https://tinyurl.com/yvr3rajs

(20) See https://tinyurl.com/wnxzmerm

(21) See https://tinyurl.com/4mrkyt55

(22) See https://tinyurl.com/f4u3khvh

(23) See https://tinyurl.com/zzm5s9pt

(24) See https://tinyurl.com/6m8mj94x

(25) See https://tinyurl.com/nyezw2ms

(26) See https://tinyurl.com/yjhkvwmw

(27) See https://tinyurl.com/4zxw2y85

(28) See https://tinyurl.com/3aaxv9ps

(29) See https://tinyurl.com/32dkczvm

(30) See https://tinyurl.com/9w3azd

(31) See https://tinyurl.com/4xkv9bcp

(32) See https://tinyurl.com/3dtfdrtj

(33) See https://tinyurl.com/y4s47nbu

(34) See https://tinyurl.com/4cb6aenr

(35) See https://tinyurl.com/z5shnm5r

(36) See https://tinyurl.com/kzt9wsve

Illusion, Delusion, and Empire

(1) See https://tinyurl.com/9vrraw8p

(2) See https://tinyurl.com/vdea9xkx

(3) See https://tinyurl.com/xphd8j3z

(4) See https://tinyurl.com/yktb2b6f

(5) See https://tinyurl.com/3ruc9ezd

(6) See https://tinyurl.com/bcmjs9vk

(7) See https://tinyurl.com/ukdxdym3

(8) See https://tinyurl.com/2vwuvvw7

(9) See https://tinyurl.com/hv2yewck

About the Author

Brant von Goble is a writer, editor, publisher, researcher, teacher, musician, juggler, and amateur radio operator.

He received a Doctor of Education degree from Western Kentucky University in 2017. During his doctoral studies, he researched the impact of motivational training on the social and emotional development of students.

.